# FEEDING TIME

## TALES OF MY CAT COMPANIONS

Steven Roesch

**author**HOUSE®

*AuthorHouse™*
*1663 Liberty Drive*
*Bloomington, IN 47403*
*www.authorhouse.com*
*Phone: 833-262-8899*

*Published by AuthorHouse 12/10/2021*

*ISBN: 978-1-6655-4571-6 (sc)*
*ISBN: 978-1-6655-4590-7 (hc)*
*ISBN: 978-1-6655-4589-1 (e)*

*Library of Congress Control Number: 2021924036*

*Print information available on the last page.*

*This book is printed on acid-free paper.*

# CONTENTS

# PREFACE

She lives alone—except, of course, that she doesn't.

That's not how it starts out, though. It starts when she takes a three-hour drive to a secluded hunting lodge with her cousin Luise and Hugo, her cousin's husband. When they arrive at the lodge, it's already three in the afternoon. Later on, at four-thirty, Luise and Hugo set off for a stroll to the village close by. Luchs, their Bavarian bloodhound, goes along with them, and our heroine enjoys the solitude and scenery they've left behind.

Then, of course, things get weird. Luchs comes back on his own; neither Luise nor Hugo appears anymore. The woman prepares some food for herself and Luchs and then settles down for the night, but in the morning it's clear that no one else has come back in the meantime.

She takes Luchs outside and begins walking toward the village. At one point she lets him take off way ahead of her. Then she hears him howling in pain, and when she catches up with him, bloody spit is running out of his mouth. She starts to go on, but he wants her to turn back and tries to block her progress. His attempts are in vain, though, and she strides on—only to knock her head into a cool, smooth, and completely invisible barrier.

So begins Marlen Haushofer's 1968 novel *The Wall*. The woman finds herself separated from the rest of the world and cut off from any certainty about what's transpired. When she goes back to Hugo's black Mercedes and checks out the car radio, all she gets for her pains is barren static.

She explores the area of land that the wall's locked her into. On the other side, in the distance, she can see an old man next to a well, a woman sitting in front of the cartwright's cottage, a German shepherd, a pair of cows. All of them are apparently dead, but it's not clear what killed them. What strikes her and makes her uneasy: the road is deserted, and no one else has apparently come around to examine this barrier and trace where its boundary is exactly.

What it is, how it was erected, what its purpose could be—none of this is evident, nor does the novel ever spill the beans. Did a top secret military weapon get deployed by accident—or maybe on purpose, by a foreign power? Have other walls sprung up elsewhere—and, if so, how many? Will this barrier be permanent, or will it vanish later on? No explanation is forthcoming, ever. Nor can she ever figure out what's happening beyond her piece of earth. Has everyone else died in some sort of unnatural catastrophe? Are there other survivors—and, if so, can she get in touch with them somehow? She has no access to up-to-date news, no information that would help her make sense of this predicament and maybe deal with it better.

Haushofer offers us a female Robinson Crusoe, someone who struggles to survive in a harsh and menacing new normal. The book takes the form of a report that she's putting together—maybe something for a future reader, maybe just a project to help her maintain her sanity, and possibly just sheets of paper that, down the line, mice will feast on.

With the advent of the COVID-19 pandemic in 2020, and especially after the imposition of a stay-at-home order in California in mid-March, I found myself flashing back to scenes in Haushofer's book. Just like her nameless character, I was abruptly separated from the larger world. Compared to what she and I had known before, this new way of living was tiny, discomforting. It was quieter in some ways, unnerving in every way.

Of course, many aspects of her situation differed sharply from mine. For starters, I could always get current news about the larger world—far too much, in fact. Day in and day out, domestic and international media served up the latest figures about the pandemic—the spiraling crises in hospital emergency rooms, the heated debates about protocols for businesses and schools, and all the rest. Also, of course, no physical wall actually surrounded my place. I wasn't literally blocked off from other neighborhoods and towns and cities. I could get outside, and now and again—though hardly as much as before—I went on brisk trips to places like the grocery store and the ATM machine.

Still, her life changes radically after that wall grew—or maybe fell—into place, and mine did too. It ushers her into a new way of existing and, over time, a new identity. It steals her future—the future that she'd imagined and expected. In a similar way the months and years that I'd anticipated weren't there anymore. The trajectory of my life had been taken away, and I wasn't sure where I was headed or where, in fact, anything was headed.

Another key similarity: her animal companions.

Now she lives alone—but actually she doesn't. She enjoys the fiercely loyal company of Luchs, a quick-witted Bavarian bloodhound, and comes to rely on him. Soon enough a cow, Bella, makes her appearance, and also a striped gray and black cat as well as the cat's daughter. These animals quickly become her family, her clan.

For my part, I found myself sheltering in place with six felines—two who tended to linger indoors, all of the others definitely outdoors types. Just like the nameless character in *The Wall*, I came to see and appreciate them in newer, more profound ways in this screwy, restricted existence.

Something else that crossed my mind a lot as the pandemic took hold: a museum exhibit that I'd visited once back in the eighties. It was in the German city of Heilbronn, and that summer morning I checked it out with Siegfried Jähne, a friend and fellow teacher.

To a casual visitor the exhibit was underwhelming at first. The museum workers had partially reconstructed several streets in the city—not the entire buildings, but just the black and white facsimiles of the fronts of the buildings and narrow streets between those facsimiles. They'd enlarged historical photographs of their facades and then artfully arranged them side by side to create the feeling of the actual 1940s streets. Pacing through them, you could see rows of small businesses—bakeries, butcher shops, stationery stores—that had been deftly brought back to a kind of surreal life. You could pass through intersections, and on occasion you saw, frozen in the blown-up photographs, shoppers and laborers going about their business in that era.

During World War II Allied bombers had attacked Heilbronn, like so many other German towns and cities. The most destructive air raid, which took place on December 4, 1944, demolished the city center and killed more than six thousand people in half an hour.

This museum exhibit aimed to recreate the look and atmosphere of some of the streets that had been wiped out on that fateful day.

While Siegfried and I made the rounds, taking it all in, an elderly man brushed past us, gazing at the two-dimensional storefronts with tears welling up in his eyes. He'd grown up in Heilbronn, he'd frequented these streets as a boy—and now, after decades of absence, here they were for him to look at again. Moving through those passages, he grew ever more distraught and heartbroken. He spoke openly—to us and to other visitors close by—about the businesses and intersections he recognized, the places that had sunk into oblivion long ago.

As news about COVID-19 unfolded, it seemed that the long-term fallout from this pandemic might spell something similar for me. All of a sudden there were stores and eateries and public spaces—favorites of mine, places I'd frequented—that were pretty much gone from my life for the time being. I couldn't go to them as I'd done before, and what the future held remained in darkness. What if this global crisis kept getting worse? To what extent would any of those haunts be available in the future?

Life as I knew it grew pale and wan; it receded and then kept on receding. Would I be like that elderly man in the museum later on, lamenting the permanent loss of places and spaces that had once been mine? Just how dire would this get, and what would the world look like later on?

On the other hand, there were the felines.

They remained constants in a kaleidoscope of changes. Not that I noticed it right away, but they became an anchor, a steady and inspirational force. Their quirks and oddities continued unabated; they were a balm in an otherwise perplexing and fearsome time. They'd nag me in their usual ways as mealtime approached, or they'd watch me with relentless fascination when I did vanilla-bland garden work—and, just by being themselves, they fed me with a gracious sense of normalcy and continuity. As other things melted into the distance and uncertainty, all of them grew in stature and in their ability to hearten and to delight.

Truth be told, I hadn't thought much about them right before the advent of COVID. Many things had become routine. Feeding them in the morning and then later in the day, taking them to the vet's office when that was called for—all of that had settled into predictable movements that I could perform with little thought and attention. Now, though, the world had become quieter, and what rose within that uncanny hush was a grander appreciation of these cats. As I—and so many others—withdrew into a more private sphere, this posse of critters took on a far more intense glow and value.

As the shelter-in-place order continued, I was trying to figure out how to deal with the new, unexpected rhythms of life as it was now. How should I live? How should I organize my time?

How to deal with the chronic uncertainty of these times—not just the pandemic itself, but the angry politics, the body blow to the economy? What I needed, I told myself, was a new project—something substantial, something that I could sink my teeth into. At the same time, though, I was casting around for something that would be uplifting, something that would serve as an antidote for the turmoil that was raging in so many quarters.

Faced with her own daunting new normal, the woman in *The Wall* eventually put together a report, one that threw the spotlight on her animal compatriots.

And so I decided to tell the stories of the cats, not just the ones here now, but also the many earlier ones who have been with me over the last thirty-plus years, and to draw inspiration and joy from that retelling.

As I began writing things down, I grew even more aware of their moods and movements, their distinct qualities and charms. Simple, everyday events came into sharper focus and held more meaning for me than ever before.

Like feeding all of them in the morning.

# FEEDING TIME

On a typical day in early 2020 things around here get going at six, when I feed the felines. All of them are pretty much outside, unless one or both of the tabbies, either Oliver or Gulliver or both, have opted to spend the night indoors for once. Wherever they are, though, they start yowling as I move around in the kitchen and especially when I delve into the cupboard and pull down a hefty bag of dry cat food.

I crack open the back door. If Oliver's out back, he wastes no time in finagling his way inside. His morning greetings are especially noisy, belligerent, and indignant. He screeches at me as he makes his way across the linoleum to get to his bowl. He might give the empty bowl some demonstrative licks as he waits for me to fill it with new fare, but mostly he's glaring at me with sharp, impatient eyes.

Once I dump a handful of munchies down in front of him, it's high time to serve the others outside. Before I open up the back door again, I give the gang a familiar signal—I rap the door three times with the back of my hands to let on that I'm coming out with their grub.

As soon as the door's open, though, there's a cat explosion: a flood of vociferous intruders bursts inside. At least three of the bunch—Johann and Maxwell, with Momo close behind—venture far into the house. They check out the whole kitchen, touch base with the scratching post in the living room, then turn tail and scurry to the back steps leading down to the garden and their assorted bowls. Moritz, the sole black cat in the lineup, awaits his breakfast atop the blue recycling container, and I always keep his bowl up there to make things easy. The others now await their turn with relative civility and cordiality—except for Johann, who's not above swiping at anyone who comes too close to him and might have designs on his early morning entrée. From time to time all of them engage in

1

energetic preprandial stretches, like seasoned runners before a marathon. And, needless to say, however speedily they get their allotments, it's never quite speedy enough to meet their discriminating standards. Soon the cohort settles down and concentrates on the serious task of eating, and their communal munching sounds, to my ears, like the rustling flow of a mountain stream.

As for Maxwell the loner, he keeps a prudent distance from the others, looking on from the safety of the lawn. It's not uncommon that I even have to search for him sometimes—where is he hanging out this time?—and then bring his dry food out to him. Only gradually does he deign to notice the bowl and its contents. For a few moments the black and white wonder feigns indifference, and only after that does he dig in and munch on his chow with abandon.

In recent weeks I've topped off Johann's bowl with a little extra something on my way back into the house—after all, a while back he got into a major spat with a neighborhood feline and garnered savage wounds on his face and neck as a result. After his appointment at the pet hospital he needed to wear an E-collar and stay inside my spare bedroom for ten days—not a comfortable situation for a freedom-loving outdoor type. At last, just a few days ago, the vet gave him a thumbs-up: the cone could be removed, and more sallies into the neighborhood are now permitted.

# WALDI

When I was growing up, nobody would have guessed that I'd wind up as a cat person. After all, my early life was dominated with the occasional presence of Noodles, a sleek jet-black dachshund who nominally resided down Midvale Road a bit, but who staked out our front door on a regular basis for affectionate greetings and the occasional tasty morsel. Later on, after Noodles met an untimely end under the front tires of a speeding car, we got a dachshund of our own, this time a tawny, wavy-haired brown puppy. Tom, my brother, had a chemistry professor named Dr. Gross; the professor's dachshund had a bountiful litter; and one of them wound up in our care and in our hearts. We dubbed him Waldi to honor the mascot of the 1972 Munich Olympics.

When he first appeared in our home, Waldi was but a tiny, befuddled pup, and he plainly missed his siblings and his familiar surroundings. The first evening he was with us we decided to keep him inside, in the service porch beside the washer and dryer, rather than outdoors or in the spartan garage. Late that night I was reading in the hush of the living room—everyone else had already gone to bed—when Waldi began whining fretfully. And whining.

I went out to keep him company now and then, but that hardly settled him down. His off-and-on racket woke up my parents and siblings, and finally we decided that I should sack out on the living room sofa, with a basket holding Waldi close by and my hand down close to him, giving him some tactile support. That oddball position seemed to mollify him, and gradually our home became his as well.

Soon Waldi became our family's soul and heartbeat, and his perspicacity about our traits and quirks was impressive. When it came to feeding him a little extra—above and beyond what he was officially supposed to get—our father was by far the weakest link in the family chain. Many dinners would find Waldi poised close to Dad's seat at the head of the table, and pieces of many a buttered roll found their way down to him over the ensuing years. Though he tried to be circumspect in these illicit feedings, our father wasn't always successful in hiding his not-so-random acts of kindness.

In the late seventies I studied at the University of Tübingen in what was then West Germany and worked part-time as an English teaching assistant in the *Uhlandgymnasium*, a local public school. During that time all I knew about Waldi came through the updates that family members sent me in their occasional letters.

When I flew back to San Francisco in the summer of 1979, my father and Ursula, my older sister, picked me up at the airport and ferried me back home to Lodi. Waldi—now a much bigger, hairier beast—waddled toward me and greeted me heartily. I spent some time in my room unpacking and freshening up, and in the meantime Waldi went to work, inspired in a way that only astute and loyal long-term pets can be. His basket in the kitchen held a jumble of stuff from each of us, and now he sniffed through his collection, located a T-shirt of mine that had fallen into the mix years earlier, and brought it to the front of my closed door. It would be hard to imagine a more moving gift than that one, and Waldi and I remained close, just as he did with everyone else in the household, during his long and pampered life.

A few weeks later I was on the cusp of leaving again, this time to Canada to study Comparative Literature at the University of Toronto.

There's a German saying that *Die Seele geht zu Fuß*: your soul travels on foot, and when you're in transit it takes some time for your spirit to catch up with your physical surroundings. Something like that afflicted me one evening before I went to Toronto. I was standing out in the backyard, gazing around at the rosebushes and the summer veggie patch and not actually seeing much at all, alone except for a mindful Waldi. He let out a husky bark and started circling around the lawn's perimeter, and soon enough I found myself going after him in hot and mindless pursuit. His jolly insistence that we indulge in play was just what I needed at that moment.

# SHIBUMI

So how did my deep-seated allegiance to cats even start? Well, it's all connected with the murky world of international intrigue.

Back in 1984 I taught a pair of summer courses at the University of the Pacific in Stockton. One of them, German for Travelers, was fairly standard fare—an introduction to useful words and phrases *auf Deutsch*. The other one was something totally different: Cloaks and Daggers—The Contemporary Spy Novel. My syllabus included novels by Deighton, Fleming, and Greene, and also a cult classic of the time called *Shibumi*, whose author concealed his identity behind the pseudonym Trevanian. The first time I'd flipped through its glorious pages the paperback held me in thrall. Its central figure, Nicolai Hel, was larger than life, an adroit and deadly assassin whose unconventional ancillary talents ranged from fluency in the Basque language to a keen fascination with an Oriental game called Go.

Preparing for the course, I felt obliged to learn about this game, and before long I fell deeply under its spell. The knowledge I picked up about Go's history and rudimentary strategy and tactics paid dividends in more ways than one. For example, it helped me understand how Trevanian had structured his novel. The titles of various sections—"Fuseki" and "Seki" among them—corresponded to aspects of Go games and illuminated the colorful goings-on in Hel's out-of-left-field life.

When the course wrapped up, my interest in Go was still going strong. I was hooked, and I needed to find venues for exploring the game further and in greater depth.

And so I began trying to track down people in the Lodi-Stockton area who also knew about Go, people who played it and could teach me more. I sought out some local Buddhist temples and posted signs with my contact information on their bulletin boards, figuring that some of their members might be aficionados. When that failed to turn up any viable leads, I kept on asking friends and acquaintances for their counsel.

Out of the blue I got a phone call one Thursday evening. A woman named Lenny introduced herself, mentioned that she'd heard about my interest in Go, and then invited me to come over to her house in Stockton to play a game or two. About a week later I drove over to her home and followed her out to her backyard, where she'd set up a table, two chairs, and a Go board with the requisite stones lying in wait. Our matches that evening were hardly even. She'd been probing the game's subtleties for several months. I, on the other hand, was a neophyte, and each game we played soon turned into a rout. Shalom, her Doberman, watched me closely—and somewhat mournfully, it seemed to me—from his post below the table.

That time, if memory serves, I didn't encounter any of her cats. This, however, was to change.

# TRIBBLE

For quite a few years my friendship with Lenny centered on Go, and on a fairly regular basis I went over to her place to match wits with her over a stone-covered board. Over time her cats took an interest in our activities—especially one furry ball with deep and watchful eyes. She'd dubbed him Tribble in honor of an especially memorable *Star Trek* episode—"The Trouble With Tribbles"—and that was the only moniker that would do him justice.

Tribble wasn't someone that Lenny had formally sought out and adopted—far from it. She'd taken to setting out munchies for strays in the neighborhood, and when this one started to show up every day and partake of her good will, his black fur and pint-sized cuteness made her next decision unavoidable. She took him into the rental and granted him status as one of its permanent co-residents. Many times during our Go battles Tribble would find his way onto my lap, a place that gradually became his power spot and makeshift throne.

Once Lenny left her front door ajar, and Tribble, spying a rare opportunity, bounded outside into the windy evening shadows. I followed him out, caught up with him at the curb, and scooped him up. To hear Lenny tell it, this was highly atypical behavior. Normally the Trib would just keep moving and evading his human pursuers—and this should have especially happened with me, a relative stranger in his network of human contacts. Clearly, then, a bond had already been established between the two of us—the first connection that I'd ever formed with a cat.

Not that I was always amiable and full of benevolence vis-à-vis the little one. Sometimes, while Lenny was pondering her next move, I'd fix my gaze on Tribble, then poke him on one side of his face. As soon as he turned his head to react to my poke, I'd tap him on the other side of his face—either that or on top of his head, prompting him to respond accordingly. Part of the fun lay in accelerating the pace of these random moves and watching his increasing irritation and fruitless efforts to parry my attacks, and also his attempts to anticipate the location of my next assault. My efforts to master Go progressed only haltingly, in fits and jagged starts, and I never really got the hang of its nuances and subtleties. On the other hand, here was a game that I could quickly master and excel at.

And things might have gone on this way, with Tribble firmly ensconced in Lenny's lively gang of feline homies.

Then came 1989.

It was the end of the summer, right before the nuts-and-bolts faculty sessions that signaled the start of a new term at my school. Lenny and I talked on the phone, and she let me know that Jerry, the man she'd been visiting regularly up in Fort Bragg, was now her soon-to-be husband. One issue hovered in the air, though, and it was a major one: Jerry was allergic to cats. Lenny's game plan was to take one or two of her felines with her when she moved to the coast permanently, his allergies notwithstanding. Some of them, though—among them, Tribble—would have to be jettisoned.

I readily agreed to take in the fuzzy black one, and Lenny threw in a scratching post that I could bring down to Fresno to help Tribble become acclimated.

One reason I didn't hesitate to accept the responsibility for Tribble was the close connection that he and I already shared. After all, not everyone will tolerate a person who repeatedly pokes him on the face and then return, again and again, for more of the same.

Another factor that led me to adopt Tribble involved one of my sophomore English students, Richard Najera. As I noted in my journal back then, *Richard…kept bugging me about Dean Koontz's* The Watchers *until I finally did read the thing.*

Getting to know that hyperintelligent golden retriever in the Koontz thriller probably inspired me, in part, to take on Tribble.

Lenny's plan to hand Tribble over to me was efficient, straightforward— and nothing short of traumatizing for Tribble himself.

In mid-August she moved her belongings out of her Stockton rental. She took the cats that would be staying with her, found suitable homes for most of the rest—and left Tribble alone in a virtually empty and silent house. She left the house key with Alicia, a mutual friend.

All I had to do was get up to Stockton, arrange to meet Alicia at the house, put Tribble into a spanking new cat carrier, and head back south to my apartment in Fresno. Nothing seemed more unproblematic. But none of us had reckoned with just how spooked and unsettled Tribble had become.

*[M]eeting with Lenny et al. on Saturday evening. I got to her house a little after seven. She was in the shower, Alicia and Tribble in the now-empty living room. Lenny had lost her wallet—the worry showed in her reddened eyes throughout the evening. We went to Shaky's Pizza along Pacific Avenue to meet up with Karen, a friend of Lenny's from her aikido circle, and Rob, a friend of Alicia's. The evening was pleasant, wholesome, full of freewheeling conversation and hearty laughs. Somehow it didn't even occur to me that this was the last time I'd see Lenny at her rental.*

Implementing Project Tribble was a lot tougher than we'd figured.

*Last night I said my goodbyes to the family, then loaded the cat carrier onto the front seat and bombed over to Lenny's place. Alicia was there already, and after sliding the giant felt scratching post into the rear of the Dasher, we went looking for Tribble. Living room? No. Kitchen? Patio? Apparently not. I was standing in the middle of the backyard searching through the weeds along the fence when Alicia called from the house: Tribble was hiding behind the stove. Sure enough, the little one was crouching back, way back, in the space between the stove and the kitchen wall, looking warily at me and the Science Diet food I was offering.*

Science Diet alone wasn't enough to lure him out into the open, even though several well-meaning people had advised me that this ploy would work for sure. The challenge was to pry him away from his hiding place, something that, given a staunch tenacity born of both fear and rage, didn't go smoothly at all. At long last I yanked him out into plain view, dropped him into the cat carrier, and secured the door—but all that only made him even more sullen and resentful.

It seemed that during the entire drive back to Fresno he was glaring at me through the slits in the carrier's side wall.

*I found myself chatting with him now and again, trying to assuage him, to assure him that he'd be in good hands, and reminding him about all the great times the two of us had spent during those epic marathon Go battles in Lenny's living room…but none of that made much of an impact on him. He hissed, he growled. His eyes spoke daggers, his eyes burned with abject fury, and he even seemed to be foaming at the mouth. I switched on 95.7 Classic Rock, hoping that the likes of Aerosmith and The Police might soothe his savage temper, but no dice.*

*About two hours later I pulled into my apartment complex in southeast Fresno. I lugged the cat carrier up the stairs to my second-floor apartment, and—after cautiously closing the door—let Tribble out of the carrier.*

The first few hours of my new life as a cat owner were hardly auspicious.

*It'll definitely take a while for him to get used to the new place. When I let him out of the travel cage, he scurried around the whole apartment, whining, looking for an open door, an open window. After hiding under my typing table for a long time, he settled down for the night underneath my bed, where he's stayed now for the whole morning. (Now it's five to twelve.)*

In the days that followed he opted to squirm under a recliner in the living room. As far as I could tell, he hardly budged from that spot for days on end.

His sojourn under the sagging recliner—something I'd gotten for free from a French teacher when I'd begun teaching in Fresno several years before—was sometimes punctuated by more outraged howls of protest, but usually wrapped in the inscrutable silence of a feline who, most likely, considered himself abducted.

I'd been naïve, figuring that the sweet, easygoing hours with this cat in the past would readily translate into a new life in this most foreign of locales—a bachelor apartment in southeast Fresno.

*I admit that I hadn't really thought ahead much about the first few days when Tribble would be down here. Somehow, though, I'd thought that the two of us would hit it off better than this. I guess that what I was looking for in Tribble—what I am looking for—is a furry companion, not a scared animal who doesn't seem to trust me or like my looks.*

Before turning in that night, I tried one more approach to make things homier for the newcomer.

*Next to my bed I've set a tray of food and water and the litter box.*

A familiar German proverb opines that *Aller Anfang ist schwer*— Everything's hard in the beginning. In this instance, though, the start was short-lived. Tribble's mood brightened much more quickly than the initial phase portended. A peripety of sorts happened just days later.

*Yesterday Tribble decided to get out from under the bed. It all happened around eight-thirty in the evening. First he stretched out his front paws a few times, allowing me to touch him a little; then he slowly pulled himself along the carpet towards me, then slipped back again toward the back wall; finally he got out, arched his back, shook himself royally, and expected to be petted. And petted. He explored more of the apartment and, by the end of the evening, made himself very comfortable—on my lap as I read my Lilian Jackson Braun crime novel and then on the scratching post between the sliding door and the "curtain" in the living room.*

*The night turned out to be noisier than I'd ever expected. He crisscrossed my bed time and time again, settling down next to my face, alongside my arms, then down at my feet. Around four he pushed his face into mine and succeeded in waking me up beyond all hope of more sleep. I ignored his meows during breakfast; at one point, though, he leaped up onto the breakfast table and almost dipped his head into my coffee mug.*

Within a few weeks an amicable phase set in and stayed put. In early September 1989, while making a journal entry, I looked *over at Tribble, who's stretched out on the window sill, still watching the gathering twilight down in the parking lot. T's made this apartment his home; he's remade my sense of it in the image of his own imagination. He puzzles over that swirling water in the toilet; he lounges for hours in the empty bathtub; he goes hunting through the closets, sniffing at boxes and textbooks, then slides behind the suitcase and makes himself very, very comfortable. Tribble's able to enjoy this existence, even when I'm not around to keep him company.*

Around that time I also wrote that his *projected name* was *"Tribble Schopenhauer."*

In my more whimsical moments T's profound, knowing stare suggested boundless wisdom and insight, making it no stretch at all to hang the name of a nineteenth-century philosopher onto his original television-inspired name. Also, *he used to pull a Schopenhauer paperback out of the bottom shelf of my bookcase...to the point that I nicknamed him Tribble Schopenhauer.*

The annual shift from summer vacation mode to full-on school and schoolteacher mode isn't always easy. Judging from my journal, though, it could well be that having this cat as a housemate now helped me make the transition with relative ease. A few remarks in August 1989 indicate as much. First, I vented about some upcoming duties that I was less than enthused about.

*There's also that blasted computer course (8 AM to 4 PM) that I'll have to take over at Fresno Pacific starting in the middle of September.*

That irascible tone changed when Tribble's name cropped up.

*Then there's Tribble—keeping him around means some extra chores, some trips to pet stores…The funny part is that nowadays I'm not fatigued. I feel ready for action, braced for a new year anew, knowing that I can get through these things and more.*

If, as Heisenberg posited, an object under observation changes its behavior, then the same holds for cat owners vis-à-vis their charges.

*I can play around with Tribble—crawling cat-like on all fours next to him on the living room carpet.*

Just like fingerprints, no two cats are actually alike, and their quirks and oddities are part of what makes them endearing. Tribble's trademark was his one-of-a-kind face push. When he sat on your lap facing you, he rarely deigned to make eye contact for very long. After a matter of seconds his stare would drift to one side or the other. If you tried to catch his stare, he'd just evade your glance again and again. Then, though, when you least expected it, he'd lunge toward you and smash his face into yours, much like a soccer pro heading a soccer ball. The Tribble face push, when it manifested itself, was a thing of special beauty—a benediction, a heartfelt blessing he bestowed on only the most fortunate and worthy, and some friends and colleagues who visited me were fortunate enough to join this exclusive club.

# Dream Place

When I decided to buy a house in the summer of 1990, the process turned out to be remarkably simple and manageable, thanks to a first-rate real estate agent that one of my colleagues had put me onto. One day the agent and I drove around to look over various properties that were currently on the market, and in the course of that day I came across my dream place. The rest was just a matter of tying up loose ends—like figuring out how to finance the purchase and also, unexpectedly, convincing the current owner, Mrs. Rogers, that, really, she wanted to accept the official selling price she was offering. Her children had been urging her to sell the house and move in with them, and she'd apparently only put it on the market to assuage them.

Several weeks elapsed before they could persuade her to go through with the sale. Once Mrs. Rogers decided, with helpful nudges from her children, to take the plunge and move in with them, everything fell speedily into place.

Actually, it wasn't so much a dream house as a dream garden. The backyard boasted a number of established and fecund fruit trees, including a proud and noble apricot tree that took center stage, and it had more than enough sunny space for the vegetable garden I wanted to get going.

Moving into the new place went without a hitch—except for Tribble, the predictable exception. Just like all cats, he abhorred disruptions in his environs and routines. Once again, as had happened up in Stockton, he witnessed his living quarters dissolving and vanishing. During this latest upheaval he couldn't squeeze into a cozy slot behind the stove, so instead he pried open a cupboard in the kitchen and stashed himself in there until, after another exhaustive search, I could track him down.

Luckily for him, the sagging recliner joined us in the new place and found a cherished position there for a time. He could hang out underneath it for quite a while—lingering in its shadowy, familiar confines until the house shed its aura of strangeness and danger.

Soon enough he adjusted to the new location, but the world beyond those safe and secure rooms proved to be a challenge, as I wrote to Lenny that September.

*Tribble is now well-adjusted to his new digs, and he really enjoys just perching on window sills and watching life unfold. When I let him into the garden, though, he's at the mercy of some of the bigger, meaner neighborhood cats. One, an unkempt brown one, likes to jump out at T. from the bushes and yell the cat equivalent of "Boo." T. of course, takes off like lightning into the safety of the house. The entrance to my crawl space is damaged, I've found out, so these same neighborhood cats are currently using the crawl space of my home as their new clubhouse.*

Within the house, as I shared with Lenny, Tribble began to stake his claim to things that he felt were rightfully his.

*Tribble, in case you had any doubts, is still very much Tribble. He's made friends with Mephisto, the cat who's been hanging out in my backyard and who's adopted me as his master. You know, Lenny, you never did tell me how temperamental and feisty T. can be. Lately he's gotten to be really territorial— for example, about my bed. I've tried to let him know that it's MY pillow, but the little one has a slow learning curve and, when irritated, a mean meow.*

# EXCHANGE

If Tribble got used to his new surroundings, though, something entirely different was percolating inside me. Somehow I'd caught another serious case of *Wanderlust*, in part because of the student exchanges I'd organized a few times with our district's partner school in Heilbronn. During those expeditions I tasted, once again, the adventurous joy of travel, and part of me hankered for something more—for a longer, more substantial sojourn in Germany, something comparable to the halcyon years of study and travel that I'd enjoyed there in the seventies.

And an opportunity to realize those impulses soon presented itself.

In the early nineties I began applying to the Fulbright Teacher Exchange Program. Getting accepted would give me the chance to teach for an entire academic year in a German school, in effect to trade my position in Fresno for a somewhat comparable one—although one teaching English—at a school in *Deutschland*. For me, at that time, it felt like a Get Out of Jail Free card in Monopoly. My work and world in Fresno had started to feel staid and predictable—probably because they were, in fact, fairly staid and predictable—and that longing for adventure and open horizons grizzled like an unruly beast inside me. Poring through Walt Whitman's "Song of the Open Road" now and then didn't quell this ambition, either, and even owning a cat didn't stop me from exploring how to make it come true.

The first time when I applied for a Fulbright luck was on my side. I was accepted, and the Fulbright people paired me up with Sigrid Theiss, an instructor from the town of Leer in northwest Germany. It looked as if all systems were go for us to swap houses and teaching posts in the fall of 1992. Then our hopes and expectations crashed and burned.

Before our exchange year got underway, Sigrid wanted to marry her fiancé, who hailed from India, but then a problem came along. The documents that he needed to get married were held up in his home country, and the wedding had to be postponed. She decided, reluctantly, to bow out of the exchange, leaving me with no option but to apply once again a year later.

Luck smiled on me a second time, though. In early 1993 the Fulbright office sent me an acceptance letter, and now it looked as if I'd be trading teaching positions with a woman who taught in a comprehensive school, or *Gesamtschule,* in Düsseldorf.

When I started corresponding with her, we probed ways of making the exchange work well. Early on I asked if she'd be willing to take care of Tribble during the year, something she wasn't sanguine about. As I found out later, the Fulbright people tended to discourage that sort of arrangement. Sometimes pets would get sick or even die during the year, precipitating feelings of recrimination or even worse. The teacher exchange needed to be based on trust and confidence, and trading anything outside of living space—cars, pets—could be problematic.

So…what to do with Tribble?

I picked up the phone and reached out to Lenny. After all, she'd been Tribble's original owner—his mom, in a way.

She gave her okay without hesitation.

That summer I was in a time crunch, struggling to get things in my house ready for the exchange and working hard to ship packages over to Düsseldorf. Only when those tasks were pretty much completed could I mull over the Tribble issue. How to pull this off exactly? How to pack him into a cat carrier and embark on that prolonged trek up to Mendocino?

Recalling the harrowing experience he'd gone through during our trip down to Fresno, I tried to get him used to being inside the carrier this time around. Now and then in the evening I'd dump him into the thing and take him on progressively longer rides around town—down toward my former haunts close to Fresno Pacific University, off toward the west, toward Highway 99 and beyond…The routine must have annoyed and bewildered him to no end. No matter—it was something that he tolerated, and it was necessary for the greater good.

On the day of my road trip with Mr. Trib it turned out to be hotter than usual—significantly hotter—and so I wound up making a pit stop at the family house in Lodi. My mother and my older sister weren't there, but

I could still take a break for a while, extract Tribble from the carrier, give him some much needed water, and let him stroll around the lush backyard lawn, using a makeshift leash made of string that I'd attached to his collar. Then it was back into the carrier, back into the VW Dasher, and straight up Highway 99 until we met up with the turnoff to Interstate 5, and from there to continue on Highway 20 at Williams. The heat was daunting enough—I could see Tribble staring at me, his eyes frantic with stress and discomfort from the disquieting temperature—but, on top of that, road work was being done here and there along Highway 20 that day, meaning that we had to stop several times and wait until the road crew waved us through. All told, it took longer than usual—8 ½ hours—to make the drive from Fresno up to Lenny and Jerry's home in Mendo.

They'd made fairly extensive preparations for Tribble's arrival—the red-carpet treatment without the actual carpet. Among other things, Lenny and Jerry had fenced in an area behind their yurt, and that was where Tribble stayed that night. As usual, I could overnight in the upper level of the round house. Ultra-early on the following morning, when rays of sunlight were streaming through the diminutive windows up there, I got dressed, found my way down the spiral staircase, and then stepped out to where Tribble stood behind the spanking new fence looking befuddled and disoriented. I sat down close to him, passed my hand over his fur. A delicate early morning calm enveloped us, and only then did it actually hit me. I was really going to do this—I'd be leaving this pal behind, way behind, for a major chunk of time, all for sake of a mushrooming *Wanderlust* that couldn't be controlled or reined in. Moments of stillness and communion, and the sort of earnest talk that you find yourself having with a cat now and then...all of it as the sunlight gathered force and purpose, and the day blossomed and asserted itself.

# Nanda

As I found out much later on, Trib's forest sojourn didn't get off to an auspicious start.

For one thing, he was used to having a litter box around in my house, and—when that wasn't readily available in his new location—he began taking a dump whenever and wherever the need took a hold of him. Once, too, he blundered his way up a tree close Jerry's and Lenny's property—and then discovered, to his dismay and mounting terror, that he couldn't get back down. All told, it took three people and an extension ladder to restore him to the clean, well-lighted place that he was gradually getting accustomed to.

His initial culture shock after being reunited with Lenny—life without a litter box, a horrific misadventure up in a tree—then shifted to a more placid and benign phase, and he settled comfortably into his new one-year home. From time to time I got updates in the mail about his condition and his status, and they painted a positive and comforting portrait of one lucky cat.

In the summer of 1994, I got back from my Fulbright year in Düsseldorf. A few days later I set out to retrieve the face-pushing one.

Now in a sleek new car, a gunmetal-gray Acura Integra, I found myself bombing along a familiar route. But just going there, fetching Tribble, and chauffeuring him back to his Fresno domicile wasn't going to be simple. Someone new had entered this particular story line, someone that I hadn't met but only heard about up to now—someone who might jeopardize the happy reunion I'd envisioned and anticipated.

Before I hit the road, I already knew the general outlines from Lenny's letters. During that year she'd worked as a volunteer at a local animal shelter and, weak-willed as she was when it came to redpoints, she decided to adopt an especially adorable one when it came onto the site. It had been attacked by dogs and, when she first laid eyes on it, was wavering between life and death. She took pains to keep him alive, which meant easing him into a shoebox and bringing him with her wherever she went.

For days she fed him from a syringe and nursed him as best she could. She christened him Nanda, and gradually the sickly little guy began to make progress. At this time she already had three other felines in her household—Chancy, Caspar, and Tribble, the temporary tenant. For whatever inexplicable reason Nanda bonded wholeheartedly and long-term with the guy from Fresno. Unexpectedly but ineluctably Tribble and Nanda now became the closest of companions, and the snapshots that Lenny and Jerry sent my way lent credence to their account.

Breaking them up, Lenny let me know, wasn't going to be an option, and she sounded inclined to keep them both. After all, Tribble had also become used to the rhythms of life in the forest, so why rock a boat that was sailing so smoothly?

She spelled out her position early on March of 1994.

*What do you mean, "a custody battle over Tribble"? Isn't possession 9/10ᵗʰ of the law? Of course, Chancy HATES him, Jerry barely tolerates the litter box, and he lives in fear here of the yellow monster (which he deals with by eating; I think he may actually be wider now than he is tall), but I adore him (when he isn't clawing my chair or the carpet or biting Chancy in the back). He spends his day sleeping by my side on my desk, and at night he sleeps on my pillow (or my head, if I am so pretentious as to attempt to claim the pillow for myself).*

*Well, I warn you now. You're gonna have to REALLY want Tribble back for me to give him up. Even Jerry has grown attached to the little guy. I wish Tribs himself could speak and cast his vote. You'll have to observe him when you get here and see what kind of changes he's gone through.*

Somehow, though, I must have been able to persuade her to let me take both of them with me. My cat carrier—the same one that had transported Trib a year earlier—now accompanied me on my new mission, and I figured that it was roomy enough for the two of them. I pulled up to the yurt along Simpson Lane, bounded up the front steps—and caught my first glimpse of Nanda when Lenny opened up. Nanda was indeed a remarkable kitten, gazing up at me from the living room carpet, radiating a gentle curiosity, his soulful eyes the same hue as the cerulean carpet beneath him.

A picture that I took a few months later captures Nanda's singular and remarkable charm.

After a brief, pleasant visit with Lenny and Jerry, it was time for me to leave and make the trek back south. In retrospect it would have been a lot better had I forked out the cash for a second cat carrier—or, better yet, a more capacious single one. As it was, coaxing both Trib and Nanda into the single carrier proved to be a unique challenge.

Tribble seemed fairly calm about the whole thing. Maybe, in the recesses of his memory, he'd retained an awareness of how things had worked out, overall, on the road trip about a year ago, but Nanda looked apprehensive and deeply unsettled. After I lifted the hatchback and loaded the carrier, I peeked into the grated opening and noticed that Nanda had now climbed on top of Tribble, his paws frantically clutching both sides of Tribble's face. Tribble, for his part, looked exasperated with this arrangement, but also prepared to tolerate it.

Lenny disappeared into the house for a while as I made final preparations for liftoff, and when she came out again it was plain that she'd been crying. Cats can have that effect on you, especially redpoints in her case.

This time I opted to head straight back to Fresno without much of a pit stop anywhere. My two furry companions were remarkably silent for the duration. Once I pulled off of Interstate 5 at the Yuba City turnoff to get gas, and as I was filling the tank I glanced through the back windshield to see how they were doing. Sure enough, Nanda was still firmly planted on Tribble's head, and Tribble's expression was the same that it had been three hours earlier.

It was almost midnight when I got back to Fresno and pulled into my driveway. I swung the carrier through the front door, plunked it down in the middle of the living room, then set its two inmates free. Both of them meandered out, a confident Tribble taking the lead. Without missing a beat, he led his new housemate around the whole place, giving him the grand tour, treating him to a thorough orientation. Somehow he still had a fairly solid understanding of the house and its furnishings—and it became ever more plain that the two had forged a deep and abiding bond with each other.

# COMPANY

Many years ago a longtime friend and colleague invited me over for brunch one Sunday morning. It was a chance to indulge in a no-holds-barred round of teacher shop talk about the goings-on at our site in particular and in the district as a whole. At one point he commented, off the cuff, that I "lived alone."

Nothing, of course, could be further off the mark.

For one thing, people who live alone leave deserted houses behind when they go out.

My place is hardly empty of life when I'm away. Also, as long as I'm inside the place, I'm dealing with my housemates, who can be as demanding and unpredictable as other humans.

Alone? So what happens when I want to withdraw into my study and deal with some pressing tasks—mundane things like paying bills or catching up on exigent correspondence? More often than not, whining and plaintive and querulous noises come from the other side of the door, and typically these are punctuated with cats' paws scratching or jabbing at the door's surface. Or the tips of those paws start to reach in underneath the door. If they were larger, they'd be paws with real horror movie potential.

At times this group will be content with just lying around, licking themselves clean ad infinitum, and—settled down in stillness—contemplating the scene around them. Other times, though, it's another story, and they're not above trailing me, harassing me, and actually bullying me if they feel the urge to do that—for example, if their collective hive mind is convinced that now it's dinner time and I should act accordingly and fulfill my duties.

The months that followed Nanda's arrival were fairly idyllic, catwise. Trib and his junior associate remained devoted comrades, and their presence and colorful antics became my new normal. During the day they'd often hang out inside, lounging here and there as the mood took them, and at night the duo went on clandestine prowls that I never learned much about. It was probably better that way.

A steady grace now filled the house, with the two felines complementing each other—authoritative heft versus diminutive sweetness, moody dominance versus innocent curiosity and wonder.

When both of them patrolled the lawn out back, Trib with his portly girth and Nanda with his brisk, youthful gait, I was reminded of Shakespeare's Falstaff and young Prince Hal, and I imagined that, in some ways, the two of them did indeed "hear the chimes at midnight."

Around that time a married couple with a cat of their own moved into the rental next door. One evening I overheard the woman over there talking to her own pet and admonishing it, "Stay away from those two! Those are the bad cats!"

So exactly how did my chums garner such notoriety?

It could be that their bad rep had to do with Nanda's seasoned hunting instinct. Before I'd jetted over to Düsseldorf, Tribble had been a fairly placid stay-inside type, having neither the opportunity nor, it seemed, the inclination to track down birds or mice and dispose of them savagely. Now, under Nanda's tutelage, he spent more hours outside, away on expeditions and adventures I couldn't begin to fathom.

One weekend afternoon I spotted Nanda pacing across the back lawn with a young bird in his mouth, openly proud of himself and his trophy. I caught up with him, teased his prey out of his mouth, and then tried, in vain as it turned out, to keep the bird alive. I set up a safe location in the garage, a cat-proof container atop the dryer, offered it different sorts of food, and used a dropper to give it water. But what exactly was appropriate food? I called around to knowledgeable people and asked for help, checked up on my patient many times…but a few hours later his eyes were squeezed shut in a mask of death.

I learned a hard lesson that day: yearn as I might, I can't stop these cats from honoring the mandates of their instincts, nor can I do much to rescue their victims once those instincts have been unleashed.

Nanda occasionally manifested an unsettling and disturbing energy, probably something that Tribble encouraged. In September 1994 I wrote to Lenny about this.

*Before you gave me Nanda, you never mentioned that he was possessed by demons. When you have time, be sure to send me the exorcism script. It'll come in handy when he's tearing through my study.*

Both cats now relished drawn-out sessions of one-on-one combat.

*It's lucky that Tribble's black and Nanda's white. That way, when they're engaged in epic brawls on the living room carpet, I can easily observe and enjoy every nuance of their paw action.*

At the end of that calendar year I seem to have accepted their character traits and my fate.

*Nanda, along with my trusty sidekick Tribble, sees to it that life around here is never too dull or predictable. Whether they're reenacting the Battle of Agincourt in the living room or just whining about my choice of cat food, they're always a pair to be reckoned with.*

The novelty of housing a pair of cats was invigorating and refreshing; on the other hand, their vicious hunting ways were unnerving. It was also just a matter of time until I'd have to deal with another unsettling aspect of pet ownership—the hammer blow of a pet dying.

# Dogs

Some cats, it seems, have a fate or destiny just as some humans do. Nanda's life was slated to be a difficult one, a life prone to accidents and calamities of all shapes and magnitudes.

When Lenny first came across him up north, he was wavering between life and death, and down here with me he ran into similar challenges. Once, within a year of his arrival in Fresno, another cat attacked him. He wound up spending three days in a local animal hospital, and when I picked him up the veterinarian was quick to let me know that his prospects were slim at best. Even after his treatment there, Nanda was a miserable, shivering ball of damp fur. When I brought him home and took a closer look at him, my next move was a no-brainer. I phoned the district's automatic teacher substitute system and took a personal day off from school.

An extra-early wakeup call got me up. I whisked over to my classroom in the wee hours of morning, left materials and instructions for my sub, and spent the rest of the day parked out in the living room next to Nanda. I placed him on top of some sheets and blankets on the sofa, and Tribble moved into position close by to provide his own tender support. Stacks of student work lay at my feet, and I went into teacher-correcting mode, checking in on Nanda behind me at regular intervals, returning to the flow of marking papers, and repeating that cycle for hours on end. Tribble did yeoman's service as a nurturing and supportive comrade, spending the entire day close by. That day marked a peripety in Nanda's prospects for recovery.

When writing *The Magic Mountain*, Thomas Mann, a Nobel Prize-winning German author, dubs his protagonist *das Sorgenkind des Lebens*—the problem child of life. Nanda filled that role in my household. This time, as on several others, he weathered the storm of calamity and moved forward to see rosier days. But it should have hit me a lot sooner that his days were numbered. Cats, we've been told, have nine lives. Given his multiple close encounters with danger and death, Nanda seemed to have ninety-nine of them, but even his good fortune was destined to reach its limit sooner than expected.

Exactly how he passed will always be a mystery. One afternoon I got home from school, and he wasn't there. The whole place felt twisted and wrong, as if I'd come into the living room and found out that all of the furniture had been spirited away. That weight of emptiness persisted, and I began looking around in the back alley and along the street and knocking on neighbors' doors. I finally got a lead from Woody, a retiree who lived kitty-cornered on Princeton Avenue. When I came over, he was sitting contentedly on his front porch, as he was often wont to do, and when I asked him about Nanda, he told me what he'd seen. A few days before, two feral dogs had come upon Nanda in the front yard and chased him up the driveway and toward the gate to the backyard—and beyond Woody's field of vision. At that time the gate wasn't locked, so if Nanda had jumped up on the wall and down into the back it wouldn't have stymied his pursuers.

And that was all that Woody knew—but it was enough, and it was plausible enough. I'll never have completely reliable, incontrovertible knowledge, but it looked as if those dogs had caught up with my cat and then disposed of him with the ferocity and skill that they'd probably used on earlier victims of theirs—and that Nanda had meted out to his own long list of victims.

Up to that time my central Fresno neighborhood had looked serene and placid, brimming with single-family homes that, all in all, were well maintained and attractive. That's part of what had drawn me to this part of town in the first place. Now, though, it held something new—an underside, a foreboding that cast a pall even in gentle daylight.

# FALKOR

When did I figure out that I needed another cat? Other people that I knew, Lenny among them, had more than one feline. Beyond that, though, my own time with the dynamic duo had been an auspicious one, something that I'd gotten used to.

Yet another factor: my occasional travels. In the summers of 1987, 1989, and 1991, I took groups of students over to Germany to spend time at our district's German partner school, the *Mönchseegymnasium* in Heilbronn. Each time that happened Tribble was confined inside the house, on his own, for the full five weeks. Although I always arranged for someone, usually my colleague Marty Radbill, to come to the house every day to tend to the Master's sundry needs, he was still visibly affected in the wake of these absences—withdrawn, moody.

I found Falkor at the SPCA Adoption Center on Hughes Avenue. I wasn't sure what sort of a cat I wanted exactly, but my gut told me to pick one that wasn't black. Little did I realize that this acquisition would usher in a lifelong affection for tabbies.

I named him Falkor, with the luck dragon in Michael Ende's fantasy novel *The Neverending Story* in mind.

When Falkor entered the picture, Tribble had been an Alpha Cat for a considerable amount of time, and it took quite a while for him to warm up to—and then cozy up to—this lively newcomer. Another discovery of mine: it turned out that the close, ineluctable bond between Tribble and Nanda wasn't the norm by far, and that many times two felines in the same household develop and cultivate a guarded respect, or an open ambivalence, or even an overt contempt for each other.

For his part Falkor was above all curious about this dark-haired creature close by, and his inquisitive nature, coupled with his outgoing verve, led him again and again to make friendly overtures toward Tribble, something which the portly one rejected just as often for a time. It looked as if my hopes of providing another buddy and brother-in-arms for Tribble would come to nothing—but I'd clearly underestimated the force of Falkor's persistence.

One of my photo albums documents what happened next.

When Falkor made dicey advances, Tribble would retreat to what, to his mind, looked like a secure location—the bathtub.

The first picture in this set shows Tribble safely ensconced in the tub, but nonetheless on high alert. For his part, Falkor is perched atop the bathroom scale, clearly eager to make his housemate's closer acquaintance.

In the second shot Falkor's posed on the rim of the tub, gazing down on the object of his curiosity, and he's reached this phase without unleashing

Tribble's ire. True—Tribble's facing away from his observer, but at least he's tolerating this proximity.

The third picture shows even more progress. Here Falkor's still on the rim, but much closer to Tribble's head, and Tribble's body language shows a relaxed and accepting state of mind.

Finally, a shot taken several days later on shows both of them in the tub, Falkor nuzzled along Tribble's substantial underside. The initial cold spell had lifted, and from now on their friendship became ever more secure and profound.

In fact, as long as Falkor was still a kitten, they could share a window sill in various rooms and monitor the house's perimeter jointly.

Of the two of them, though, only Falkor made it a habit to clamber up one of the privets and onto the roof, where he could take stock of his turf and bask in the sun. He wasn't quite the flying dragon in Ende's novel, but he clearly venerated high places and the perspectives that they afforded him. The name I'd chosen for him had been a prescient one.

Soon the two of them pretty much reprised the previous Tribble-Nanda partnership and spent time prowling around the neighborhood together. At times their eagerness and impatience to get outside even became annoying. They'd crowd next to the back door in the early evening hours, fastening their combined gazes on me and begging me to let me them explore the Great Beyond.

Falkor, by far, hankered to get out much more than his older comrade. Of all of the cats I've housed, fed, and cherished, he was the keenest on escaping into the outside world. He honed his crafty habit of lingering close to one of the doors so that if I chanced to open it—to get the mail, to bring in the laundry—he'd burst out in a flash, then bolt over the lawn to the back fence next to alley. He'd leap up, grab the top of the fence with his front paws, and—superb athlete that he was—pull himself up. Once he was perched on top, he'd contemplate the alley out back for a moment, then bound down to go off on yet another expedition.

# AUGSBURG

*Wanderlust,* the deep-seated yearning to travel, never really vanished from my spirits, and as the new millennium started it made its presence felt inside me once again. My Fulbright year had hardly been a walk in the park—it'd been a challenging stint, in fact, with lots of rambunctious students and daunting challenges in an urban school setting—but the thrills of actually living in Europe again blew me away. It had worked out once, and the current conditions at my school made a second teacher exchange a real possibility. Some key administrators, including our assistant principal, were open to letting me take advantage of the Fulbright program a second time, and I could ill afford to pass up this favorable constellation of factors.

I took the plunge, despite misgivings about leaving not one but actually a pair of felines in the lurch for what would amount to a full year. Late in 2001 I began to fill out the application for a 2002-2003 Fulbright position, and this time around the process was far smoother and much less intimidating.

Second thoughts began to emerge in early February after I sent off the application forms.

*It's almost ten o'clock on a Monday evening. It's been a holiday, so no school and lots of time for the trifles that make life worthwhile—planting rows of Swiss chard and radishes in the garden, taking a walk through the neighborhood, peddling furiously for twenty-two minutes on the old reliable exercise bike right here behind me...Also: petting Tribble and Falkor and enjoying their company, their quirks, their wondrous friendship.*

Reflecting on the fearsome twosome led to some surprising ruminations in my journal.

*I know that the Fulbright people will probably find someone soon with whom I could, might, maybe even should trade a life and a teaching position for a year. The problem that's emerged, though, is how much I'm attached to these felines, Tribble especially. It could well be that the lasting lesson of my application for a second Fulbright is merely and unexpectedly this: that my connection with Tribble and Falkor is far deeper and more meaningful than I've ever admitted to myself.*

There were the pros, and then there were the cons. I began wrestling with the warring factions deep inside me. Part of my yearning to go—to get out of Dodge, and as far away as possible—had to do with a powerful romantic relationship that had appeared without warning and then, equally without warning, gone south. I felt the overwhelming need to get some distance between myself and this city, this work site, this fairly frozen set of life habits and routines, and break out into something new and charged with possibilities. A move like that spelled freedom, and opportunity, and also a fresh beginning of sorts.

*At this point I feel torn inside—something I never anticipated—about the prospect of going to Germany for a year. At the same time I feel torn about the prospect of staying here for another year, and a year after that, and several more years until I can retire with benefits. All that's keeping me from saying a resounding Yes to another year of adventure and surprise in Deutschland is a black bundle of longing and camaraderie that's reclining on my bed as I write this, and his pal.*

Who would have figured that two little felines could wield this kind of clout?

*It might be that Tribble and Falkor have become especially and poignantly important to me as objects of warmth and companionship. On the other hand, it could well be that this connection with my pets has emerged to "threaten" my plans for a temporary escape from the intrigues and narrowness of my work site. After all, for years I've been calling them my boys, my sons, and it could well be that my language has betrayed more than I realized or wanted to recognize about the depth and strength of my feelings for them, and maybe for this place in Fresno, too…*

*So…what to do? It seems so foolish, so all-too-human, to be obsessing because of this business. What to do with the cats if I go? How to deal with life at the school if I don't? It's as if, whatever I choose when the Fulbright envelope arrives in a matter of weeks now, I'll feel pangs of regret and misery.*

At last I reckoned that *I'll be able to deal with whatever I choose, whatever comes my way.*

Other news and events around that time did little to clarify the direction that my life should take.

*Yesterday Lenny emailed me that Caspar* [one of her cats] *has a terminal condition; she's taking first-rate care of him, but slowly, inexorably, he's facing a long goodbye. This evening, taking a walk up to First Street after posting some letters in the mailbox on Blackstone and Clinton, I spotted one cat after another, and found myself feeling the yearning and nostalgia that I'd feel if, in six months or so, I'd be in Germany alone and without my two furry compatriots.*

A conviction that I really, really wanted to dive into a second exchange year—the mindset I had when I filled out the forms and tossed them into the mailbox—had now shifted into ambivalence, hesitation, even queasiness.

*What to do? Am stunned that, at this point, I have no idea how I'll react when the Fulbright letter comes. Am intrigued and humbled, once again, to recognize just how little I recognize about my own wants and needs and inner workings.*

Once the acceptance letter came early in 2002, though, all of those second thoughts subsided and vanished. Now I held a palpable offer in my hands, something starkly real. No longer was it just an abstract thing that I could kick around inside my mind. It had become concrete, and it gave rise to a fireworks display of reverie, magical and enticing. The watchful, loving eyes of my two feline homies were still upon me, but now this exchange was something that I couldn't resist or push aside any longer.

Or could I?

*It's hard to define what's going on inside of me. Part of me feels rising tension and anxiety about this trip, about the year that's looming ahead of me. Back in 1993 I looked forward to Germany and the opportunity to teach there because I thought that the German school system was vastly superior to what I'd been experiencing in Fresno. This time around I have no such illusions.*

Once again the daunting challenges of a teacher exchange hovered in front of me, and the shadows of the unknowns were also making themselves felt.

When I began corresponding with Karin Wiedenbauer, my exchange partner in Augsburg, she didn't immediately agree to take care of the cats during her time here. I began casting around for a back-up plan in case her hesitation flipped into an outright no.

Bringing both of them to a long-term cat hotel and paying for their room and board there became a real option, and I started visiting some sites that had golden reviews. I checked out several of them, saw what they had to offer—and found out firsthand what my two would be missing in terms of mobility and other creature comforts if I were to take that route. Given his own strident *Wanderlust*, Falkor would be especially ill-suited to this type of claustrophobic lifestyle.

*Could I stomach the knowledge that the two of them were being warehoused in Elaine's Animal Inn, if that Plan B shifted into Plan A?*

*It's getting late (10:30 PM); I suppose I'll clean out some cabinets in the bathroom, maybe even stay up to look at Leno's monologue on* <u>The Tonight Show</u>*. Tribble just got up and bounded down from the computer table; maybe he somehow sensed that this entry is winding down, coming to its inevitable close...*

*It may be that, once again, just like so many times before, what I really want is another identity, an opportunity to escape myself for a time, a way to wiggle out of my life. It's as if this life—driving around Fresno, pulling into familiar parking spaces and standing at all—too—well—known store counters— has drawn too close, like a needy lover, and I've got to get some space, some distance, to uncover and really see the life that lies beyond the edges of this one.*

# Tumor

When you're playing chess against a suitable opponent, you never see all the angles. Again and again surprises come your way, moves that sweep the game along a wholly new trajectory. And life often unfolds in the same bewildering way.

I'd taken for granted that the life I was leading was a stable one. After all, it looked and felt that way. Tenure in a large school district in California, a house I owned and had now paid for completely—how could all of this not be secure and dependable? Couldn't I count on this framework to remain intact for a mere year?

When you have multiple cats, you don't necessarily realize that one of them has been eating less—or not eating anything at all. If one feline leaves something untouched in his or her bowl, a peer is apt to finish that food and, in effect, destroy the evidence.

It took me a few days to notice that Tribble wasn't chowing down anymore like his usual gluttonous self. Then it became painfully clear that something was seriously wrong. One evening after dinner he wandered into my study, struggled to jump onto my chair, and then worked twice as hard to get himself from the chair onto the desk. Simple maneuvers like these had never been a challenge for him before. Picking him up, I noticed just how much weight he'd lost and how anxious he was.

I brought him out to my regular animal hospital along King's Canyon Road, where, among other things, the vet took a blood sample from Tribble's neck, something that irked him and seemed to pain him to no end.

Whatever that vet recommended didn't improve things, and my flight date in mid-July was edging ever closer. I wanted to make sure he was in decent shape again before I took off for another year abroad. Tribble needed to get his health back, and Karin Wiedenbauer shouldn't be saddled with a sick cat.

I found someone who examined Tribble more thoroughly than the first one had, and soon afterwards I journaled about that appointment.

*The day before yesterday I took Trib to a new vet, a Sikh whose office lies along Shaw Avenue, west of Highway 99. The vet found a lump in Tribble, took an X-ray, and determined that he had something large and suspicious, possibly a tumor, in his intestines.*

Surgery was called for without delay.

*I scribbled my signature on some forms; he operated; and later that day I came by to find a confused but vocal and lucid Tribble, sporting an E-collar, sitting in a cage in the clinic. He looked healthy, definitely over the worst of it.*

The vet felt that Tribble should spend the night in the clinic to recover thoroughly and said I should plan on picking him up on the following day.

The next afternoon, after a helpful session with my chiropractor, I swung by the vet's office once again, expecting to find a cat that was even closer to full recovery.

A few days later I wrote about what came next.

*When I got there, the woman behind the desk told me that they'd moved Tribble to the incubator because he'd lost body temperature. She also seemed hopeful and positive about his chances; apparently Tribble had been moving just ten minutes before. But it was pretty clear, when she opened up the plastic lid of the incubator and I could reach inside, that something was wrong. First, there was no response to my touch whatsoever; second, there was the blank, eerily steady look (or nonlook) in his eyes. It was as if darkness had overtaken his eyes. There was no focus, no thought or reaction. She tried to take a pulse, found none, and phoned the doctor, who came in maybe ten, maybe fifteen minutes later. Before she left, she closed the lid of incubator, and through the curved plastic of its lid, peering down on Trib, I saw or thought I saw movement—the heave of the stomach, the quivering of fur—but then I realized again and again that it was only my hoping, maybe my own quivering.*

*When the vet came, he lifted the limp, lifeless non-Tribble out of the incubator, told me about the medications they'd given him that morning, about the baby food they'd tried to feed him. I asked about cremation. He said he'd be able to arrange it, that he'd knock the cost for the cremation off my bill, that I'd definitely be able to pick up Trib's ashes before I left for Germany.*

Earlier in the year, when I was up in Mendocino, Lenny's friend Benny had presented me with a bottle of very potent aquavit.

*Later, after I got home, I polished off the aquavit that Benny had given me, plus two beers, before trying to sleep.*

Something else I did was call to mind images of Tribble—a roll call of memories and moments—and journal about them.

*It seems that they should be endless, that the memories should surge on and on like the tide onto the shore, but somehow there don't seem to be enough for all of the years, the days, the wonders of that cat's life. I remember how he used to jump up onto the sofa next to me, or the armchair, and sit next to me while I read, or at least tried to read…Maybe most of all I remember so many summer nights like this one, when he'd insist on lying on the window sill, watching and presiding over the backyard, maybe while a breeze was calling across the grass and the roses were nodding and waving in reply. How he sometimes stood in the middle of the kitchen floor looking at me imploringly, disturbed, beside himself with disbelief, when I fed him something that wasn't, in his view, enough, or not the kind of grub he preferred that day.*

*It's so hard and daunting to reconcile those memories with the fragile, limp thing that was lying on the operating table after the vet pulled it out of the incubator. For starters, Tribble had lost so much weight: on his day of dying he was no longer the hefty contender, the Sherman tank. Luckily, though, his fur was still Tribble fur, and I could touch him and stroke him and run my fingers along his length before I left.*

*I remember emailing a former girlfriend in November 2000 that I was shocked to realize how fragile our connection was, how quickly it could all come unraveled. Tribble's life—his breath, his paw placed on top of my hand, his love of the lamp on the bedside table and its serene warmth—all of that was fragile, too. Since Trib lived with me, since he was as much a part of my daily routine as brushing my teeth or daydreaming or washing the dishes, his death is itself deadly, stunning.*

*Looking at that nobody lying there, first in the incubator and then later on the surgery table and then later when he was on the metal grid in another room of the clinic, I thought about how half-baked and fanciful images and explanations of the afterlife really are. You can't look in the face of death. Just like this non-Tribble's expression, death has no face that registers your existence, nothing that you can talk to. This nonface is like the mountain facades I saw in Canyonlands and Arches last summer: they have their own mighty, distant reality, and it's nothing that ever touches on yours.*

Downing my third or fourth schnapps glass full of aquavit late in the evening, I began thinking, blindly and obsessively, that I didn't like this world at all anymore.

*If the world is a place where people and pets grow old and perish, where there's so much injustice and existential ugliness and plain unfairness, then I don't know how to go on and I don't know how to face another sunrise with more duties and chores and noises tugging at me. It's as if you want to wrestle with life, to call this mad rush of events and turmoil on the carpet for doing what it does, for neglecting so much and screwing up so much. But you can't wrestle with a phantom. Your thoughts can't wrestle with something or someone anyway.*

And then I landed on the small and grand things to be grateful for. It would have been far worse to have gone to Germany and heard the news about Tribble's death from afar. Or suppose I'd gone to Augsburg and returned, only to find Tribble suffering and close to death, or to see him die just a few weeks or months after I'd come back? Or imagine that I'd have to consent to have him put down and witness that? This way I was able to be with him close to his end, to gain some closure of sorts, to witness that thought-shattering mystery of nonlife.

Those who don't own pets can't fathom the amount of trauma that a pet's death can invoke and mobilize. And how could they? Until this happened, I was clueless myself. Years ago, my close friend Marty Radbill lost Aki, his beloved collie, and his grief was profound. More recently two other friends of mine have lost cherished cats, and ever since both have shied away from getting other cats. Both keep pictures of their lost loved ones in prominent places in their homes, and their faces still shift into melancholy when they recall them. There's a cruel shock that slams down on you when a pet expires. It's not pretty, it's not fair, and the grief isn't mainstream cinematic grief. It doesn't fade out after a few intense moments of screen time.

Nonpet people might assume that, since pets are relatively small, their place in your life is also a modest one. But long-term animal companions take on a status that belies their physical size; they become soul mates and confidants in a way that few other humans can.

Several days later I was still confronting Tribble's absence.

*It's close to a quarter past ten this evening. I settled the bill with the pet hospital this morning, also picked up the cat carrier that I'd left there earlier in the week. The woman behind the counter—the first person I'd seen and spoken with on Tuesday when I brought Tribble in—said she'd do what she could to make sure that I could get the ashes from the cremation before I left the country on the 23rd. I gave her Marty's number in case the ashes would only be available after that.*

*It's not easy to explain how Tribble's passing has affected me and also not affected me. It's not as if I've frozen into some static feeling of mourning. I've continued to prepare for Augsburg—sorting through clothes, tossing old videocassettes that were in the living room and putting reusable cassettes into the garage with the other reusables—but with a certain mindfulness of the commonplace: the clouds gracing the morning sky, the buzz of afternoon traffic coming over from Blackstone Avenue.*

And then there was Falkor.

His bewildered looks and behaviors during these days dialed up my own lingering sorrow. A hunter by nature, now he was hunting for his longtime companion, and he wasn't willing to give up easily.

After Tribble passed, Falkor was visibly shaken and distraught. Trib had already been away from the house for a few days because of his operation, but of course all Falkor registered was his bro's absence, not the reasons for it.

*Often Falkor stands at the back door, wanting—apparently—to go out. When I open the door, though, he just stands and peers out into the garden, looking for a Tribble who isn't out there, either. When Marty came over for a pizza lunch, Falkor did something along the same lines: he came in and began, almost systematically, to check out all of the rooms. Usually he's been a silent cat, unless he was especially hungry or impatient with me. Nowadays he's full of anguished meows. Once this morning he went out into the garden and checked out the places that Tribble especially liked to frequent—the plants along the back wall, the cover of the crawl space…All in all, he's spending a lot of his hours indoors now, often close to the back door. Maybe it's cool in this part of the kitchen—the temperature in Fresno soared up to 108 degrees today—but maybe he also thinks that Tribble will have to saunter over to the litter box or wander over to the food sometime.*

When Tribble didn't reappear, he took to positioning himself in spots around the house where, he reasoned, Tribble would soon materialize, and there he kept a patient, watchful eye for hours at a time. One such lookout post was right behind the food bowls in the kitchen—a superb choice, given the epicurean's deep appreciation of his meals. I tried to comfort Falkor, holding him and—as cat owners tend to do—leveling with him about Tribble's demise.

*Falkor's actions bring out my own feelings of mourning and emptiness. This evening I fed him alone, carving out a part of "salmon dinner" from a tin can to spoon into his bowl. Talking with him about his food, my voice cracked.*

It dawned on me that a part of me wanted to hold on to this numbness— not so much to freeze grief as to freeze time. Time was moving forward, and me being drawn into its current seemed like a betrayal of the closeness and loyalty that I'd had vis-à-vis Tribble. His loss had plainly shaken my sense of the world and my understanding of my place in that world.

*To my left there's only a lamp, not an overweight feline full of tenderness and needs. Around me is a world that I don't understand, one I don't want to accept, one that often scares me. All of this is hurdles I thought I'd leaped over long ago, but I'm wandering through this maze again, looking for an exit that should be as familiar and ubiquitous as a stop sign. It's like what happens when you meditate. There's the ongoing task of returning to the breath, the intended focus of one's thought, and to an enlightened appreciation of the moment.*

Tribble's cremated remains now fill a miniature wooden casket in the glass cabinet next to my dining room table. Adorning it is a miniature *Star Trek*-inspired "Tribble" stuffed animal, one that Keila Benefield, one of my German students, gave me right before winter break one year. It looks like a messy clump of faux fur, but that's deceptive. Yank on the string and it starts to vibrate and throb, just like one of the tribbles in the TV episode.

# RETURN

An ultra-early morning wake-up call—time for me to get over to Germany yet again for the advent of a second Fulbright exchange year. My flight itinerary was slated to take me first from Fresno to San Francisco, and that flight was scheduled to start long before sunrise—meaning that Marty tapped on my front door at around 3 AM to get me out to the airport. I was already primed to get going, but, using some feeble excuse, I took Falkor out into the darkness of the kitchen and held him close to me, trying to let him know through touch what I couldn't render with language.

Now that Tribble had disappeared, skipping town had an entirely different weight and force. Leaving Marty behind—we said our goodbyes before I brought my bags into the terminal—was also a rough moment, since he'd been suffering from clinical depression for several months.

In fact, a lot of unexpected events haunted and unsettled me during those days, things that led me to notice, more strongly than I'd sensed for quite a while, how tentative and fleeting everything truly is. Marty had been battling depression for months, and he wasn't fully free of its hideous shadows yet. Sometimes, when he came over to visit, we'd sit outside in the shade of the apricot tree and try to talk, but the words we used sputtered and struggled. Usually our talkathons were an easygoing flow of yarns and wisecracks, but now there was a distance between us. Lenny, who'd brought Tribble and then, later on, Nanda my way, had recently been diagnosed with a brain tumor, and the outlook for her case was far from clear. How would these people's lives go on? What would happen to them?

After the plane touched down in San Francisco, I had to make my way through the hushed and darkish corridors of a terminal being renovated. While I was en route to my connection, I passed by what had been the old Lufthansa counter. I knew it well: it was where I'd started various sallies over to Europe on my own on many occasions, and—what was more poignant and heart-wrenching—it was also where I'd brought three groups of high school students in the summers of 1987, 1989, and 1991 so that we could wing our way over to Germany and spend time with our hosts in Heilbronn. Now that counter lay neglected and ready to be dismantled—another palpable reminder, as if I needed another one, of the daunting evanescence intrinsic to all our lives.

My Fulbright Exchange partner, Karin Wiedenbauer, moved into my house in the late summer of 2002; she'd agreed to shoulder the responsibility of caring for Falkor.

Early on during our exchange she sent me a photo that showed Falkor lying placidly atop the recliner in the living room. Fittingly, he was just below the framed "luck dragon" print that my mother had brought back with her from China after her travels there.

I flew back to Fresno at the tail end of July in 2003.

*The flight back to the States is a blur in memory, an almost interminable whirl of thoughts and waiting. When I landed in Los Angeles, I went speedily through customs, then noticed that an earlier flight to Fresno would be available. A shuttle bus took me over to a separate terminal, where the two women behind the counter assured me that yes, there was a seat available on that flight, and yes, I could board immediately. I needed to go to a restroom, figured I could go during the flight…and found out there was no restroom on board this commuter plane. No matter: in about an hour I was back in Fresno, emerging into a spacious new, totally unfamiliar terminal, then waiting for a taxi outside in the dusty heat. Bombing back toward my neighborhood, I felt the city's personality descending on me again. Getting to the house, I noticed how rundown and dispirited the yard seemed, especially the forlorn branches of the apricot tree.*

The whole backyard looked wilted and forsaken on that sweltering afternoon. The six tomato plants that Karin had set out in the back clearly weren't going to survive much longer; only the wooden stakes she'd plunged into the earth beside each plant looked firm and healthy. The plants themselves sagged and drooped, and looked pretty much beyond repair.

I unlocked the back door, brought my luggage inside. The house seemed desolate. There was no evidence at all that Falkor was still around at all, and the place recalled the stillness in Lenny's empty rented house when, years earlier, I'd slipped inside to fetch Tribble. Unlike Tribble, though, Falkor hadn't found a refuge behind the stove. Instead he'd scrambled underneath my bed—way underneath, where he was cowering and whimpering with mounting fear as I got closer. At first he didn't recognize me at all, and he stayed put where he was.

Getting back into his good graces took several days.

*Many lights weren't working. At first I figured a fuse had gone out, and then it hit me that the bulbs just needed to be replaced. Marty picked me up later on so that we could hit an ATM machine and then have dinner, on me, at a Carrows up on Shaw Avenue, then pick up my late-arriving luggage at the airport. I had the Acura brought over to Downtown Auto, where they resuscitated her for about two hundred bucks, and internet-ordered a new CD player and radio combo to replace the one that, somehow, had gotten itself damaged. (Coffee spilled on top?)*

One of Falkor's power spots during my absence had been the top of the recliner in the living room; I discovered another one when I checked out the Acura and found a pile of cat fur covering the back seat. One of the windows was rolled down halfway, and he'd exploited that to access the car's interior and set up his own quiet, isolated digs in the murky cool of the garage.

# Ramses

In a sense I was back home again, but in reality I wasn't quite there yet. For me home had come to mean a pair of cats, not just one.

In April 2004 I drove out to the adoption center on Hughes Avenue to find a sidekick for Falkor. For a while I waffled between two tabbies, finally settling on the one that seemed perkier. The name they'd saddled him with—Toby—didn't sit well with me, and I wasn't sure what else to call him. It didn't rattle me much, though. Apt names for the new additions always had a way of turning up in short order.

Sure enough, the matter was settled once the two of us got home. The new one strutted out of the cat carrier and then, without a moment's hesitation, toured the living room as if he owned the whole spread. When he came upon the bedroom, he leaped onto the bedspread and adopted the pose of the Egyptian Sphinx, fixing a brilliant and unflinching gaze on me.

His haughty, penetrating stare became a staple around the house from then on.

From that moment he went by the name of Ramses, in honor of Ramses II of Egypt.

This time around the cats hit it off from the get-go. They became fast friends and soon divided their hours between outside and inside, adventure and repose.

They weren't the only ones with a yearning to explore new terrain, though. In the summer of 2005 I signed up for a study tour of western Turkey, and my gut told me that it would be better for the cats to stay inside for the duration. But how to do that? Falkor was especially quick on the draw when it came to getting into the big outdoors whenever the opportunity arose, and Ramses was his adept and willing pupil. If someone came into the house during my absence to tend to their needs, they'd both be out straight away.

I'd already been restricting their outdoors activities, hoping that this would help them to transition more easily into a strictly indoors routine for the next few weeks.

*The two of them spent the night inside, something that already wasn't to their liking. Today Falkor voiced his discontent, something he usually doesn't do, about being cooped up. When I stepped outside to do some watering, their buddy, a black cat with gleaming eyes, was sitting on the lawn close to the back gate, watching me, wondering where his nocturnal companions had been.*

I shared my concerns about Falkor and Ramses with Bruce Ratcliffe, one of my colleagues at school, and later on that day he came by with a sketch he'd put together. He'd cooked up something that could allay my anxieties and keep the two penned up in the lion's share of the house. After I gave him the go-ahead, he built it for me in his garage-workshop, and the day before my flight he brought it over and installed it.

*Bruce came over yesterday with a contraption made of a wooden frame and chicken wire. It'll be held in place with clamps to prevent the cats from reaching the front door when someone enters or exits.*

He set it up between the vestibule and the living room. The person helping me with the cats would be able to come in through the front door, then close and lock that door before undoing the chicken-wire shield and getting into the rest of the house.

The Ratcliffe barrier looked a bit odd, to be sure, but it worked well. Eventually, I'm sure, the felines even came to forgive me.

# Eyes

Strictly speaking, the final day of school isn't a day of school at all.

Very little learning, if any, takes place. Only a handful of students actually shows up. The special schedule also doesn't lend itself to actual teaching. Each period might only take up twenty or twenty-five minutes, not enough time for meaningful instruction. The students who appear might busy themselves with signing yearbooks, although that task has usually been taken care of; yearbooks were distributed and available a few weeks back.

And so it was relatively easy for me to get a thumbs-up from my principal, Jim Bowen, to leave early on the final school day in June 2006. Liselotte, my mother, needed to get to the San Francisco airport that evening, and I was her designated driver.

My students spent their time in class playing board games or playing with their phones. Some just stared out the window into the quad. After the truncated schedule came to its long-anticipated end, I packed up my case, dumped it into my cart, and wheeled it out into the back parking lot before jetting home. Once there, I grabbed a quick lunch before bombing up Highway 99 to Lodi. I needed to pick Liselotte up and whisk her over to SFO.

Everything went like clockwork, thanks to her typical orderliness when it came to packing her luggage as well as my sister Ursula's scrupulously marked road map, which showed me the best route to take.

I brought several audiocassettes along for the trip—back then my Acura still had a cassette player. We checked out some pre-classical composers, mostly Corelli and Locatelli, and chatted only now and then. She seemed to be preoccupied with her trip—her requisite visits with friends and relatives in Munich as well as some solo excursions down into Italy.

Ursula's driving instructions worked well, and they took us past Hayward and toward the San Mateo Bridge. It was already late in the afternoon, sunlight was slanting down towards us, and when we were heading west it slammed into the windshield. Liselotte complained that the light was irritating her. I snapped down the sun visor on the passenger side, which seemed to make things easier for her. At the time I didn't think much more about it.

Everything went without a hitch at the airport—snagging a parking place, huffing it to the American Airlines counter, and then seeing my mother off before she went through the security checkpoint and toward her boarding gate. Liselotte was a seasoned traveler, pretty much up there with the George Clooney character in *Up in the Air*, and she knew her way around San Francisco International as well as she knew all the arias of Verdi's major operas.

When she got back from her trip, I was waiting for her in the terminal, and she looked full of energy and new stories she needed to share.

On the way back to Lodi, though, she confided to me that, now and then during her travels, her eyes had bothered her the way they had on the San Mateo Bridge. We agreed that I could make an appointment for her with my own eye doctor in Fresno, Raymond Mulvey.

A few weeks later, in July, she came down to Fresno, and I brought her over to Dr. Mulvey's office. Soon enough she was done with her appointment—but Dr. Mulvey wanted to speak with me privately.

It turned out that the pressure inside her eyeballs was unusually high— so high that his instruments couldn't even measure them exactly. The threat of imminent blindness was acute, and Mulvey had arranged for us to meet with a colleague of his, Kevin Kummerfeld, for emergency surgery that afternoon. We had to wait for quite a while at Dr. Kummerfeld's office on S Street, but later his assistants brought us in and he used laser surgery to help alleviate some of the eye pressure. That procedure, though, was just the beginning of a months-long process to safeguard her eyesight. It entailed a series of pre-surgery visits to Dr. Kummerfeld's other office on Herndon Avenue, sessions which, all told, spanned several weeks. Following that was the actual surgery—one procedure for each eye—and finally a row of follow-up sessions.

There was no way around it. Liselotte would soon need to move down to my place in Fresno for about two-and-a-half months.

And it looked like she'd have to consort with my cats.

# Voice Mail

Around that time Falkor disappeared.

*The past week and a half have been pretty intense. Falkor, for starters, went AWOL around July 11<sup>th</sup>, and even though I've spoken with neighbors and scanned the <u>Fresno Bee</u> classified pages and gone to the animal shelter three times now, he's yet to be found.*

Sometimes a cat vanishes and you never know what happened exactly. That was the situation with Nanda: all I was left with was Woody's observations, which gave me a general sense of how he'd likely met his end.

Falkor's case was different from all of that.

Early one day there was a message on my answering machine, a trembling woman's voice. She didn't leave her name, but she let me know that, when she was leaving for work that morning, she'd spotted a cat that "had expired." A car had run it over in front of her house. Falkor's contact intel was fastened to his collar.

She lived along Harrison Avenue, more than two miles away from my place, and I sped over there right away to take a look. I drove south on Fresno Avenue, hung a left on Harrison, and slowed to a steady crawl, scanning the block for something, anything. I was drawing a blank, so I U-turned and did scan 2.0, then decided to get a closer look on foot. It took a while to find a parking place, and even then…nothing.

Then I spotted him. Someone had moved Falkor's body off the street and onto the curb strip along the south side. His eyes were open but frozen, and the blow from the car had slit open his stomach and thrown his intestines into view. I'd brought along some plastic garbage liners and used them to pick him up and bring him back to the trunk of my car. Rigor mortis had already set in, and the Falkor I'd known was already far, far gone.

Once home, I grabbed the shovel and prepared his grave. Given the collision of feelings inside me it felt good, and right, to be wielding that shovel and crafting his final resting place.

The irony of his death hit me hard.

Falkor had always been sure of himself, brimming with confidence. When he lifted himself up onto the top of the back fence, or when he took advantage of a lapse in my attention to sneak outdoors, he radiated self-assurance and mastery. It was hard to square that spirit with this stiff, expressionless thing in front of me now.

What also puzzled me: How had he lost his way? How could it be that he'd wandered away from his regular beat and wound up so far from home base? It had been about two weeks since he'd vanished. How had he survived during all of that time? Did some strangers help him out, or did he subsist on plants and the odd slaughtered beast?

Halfway through that morning I headed toward the downtown library, more to distract myself than for any other reason. There, in the stacks, I came across Peter Brigham, who taught art at my school, and before I knew it, I shared what had happened. Back home, still shell-shocked—or Falkor-shocked—I called Marty, who'd known and admired Falkor as much as I had, and broke the news to him. He came over right away and gave me a full-on hug—not his usual style—and let me talk more about Falkor's life and sundry exploits.

At few days later I wrote down some salient memories *just call to mind some of the moments and qualities that made him shine:*

> *the quality of his fur—not soft like Ramses', but hair like the bristles of a brush; the way he used to leap up onto the frame of the back fence, reach up to grab the top of the fence, pull himself over, and saunter down the back alley—elegantly, athletically;*
>
> *the way he used to lie on top of my stomach and gaze at me, sometimes taking a swipe at my neck and chin for the heck of it;*
>
> *the early-morning stretching that he and Ramses undertook as a matter of course before they started chowing down their breakfast;*

*the way he almost always nudged Ramses to the side at mealtime and commandeered some of his brother's food for himself;*

*the way the two of them often went out into the back and then paused at the foot of the steps, surveying their domain;*

*how scared he was when I came home from Augsburg about three years ago; he was crouching under the bed, trembling, anxious;*

*the way he acted after Tribble didn't come home after the surgery; he insisted on touring the backyard again and again, checking out the places that Tribble had frequented, and later on he sometimes parked himself in the kitchen next to the washing machine, a spot which let him monitor the litter box and the water and food bowls all at the same time;*

*his favorite spots out back—sunning himself mornings under the rosebushes along the western fence, perching atop one of the trash bins or one of the shrubs next to the garage door, or lying on the lawn, on his stomach, back legs stretching out far behind him;*

*the effort it took grab him and lower him into the cat carrier, or to squirt the flea treatment onto the nape of his neck once a month;*

*how one morning, before going to school, I flung open the back door to spy Falkor and Ramses feasting on the entrails of a mouse they'd just killed, munching heartily, self-satisfied and mightily pleased with themselves;*

*years ago, the afternoon appointment that Falkor and I had at the veterinarian's office along Kings Canyon Avenue, when a group of children spied him in his cat carrier and insisted that I take him out; they petted him, spoiled him, handed him around the whole circle of the waiting room crowd.*

# LISELOTTE

Ramses might now have been the sole cat on my premises, but soon enough a new housemate came along—Liselotte, who needed to continue her eye treatments with Dr. Kummerfeld. Ursula helped her pack for the drive, and she did yeoman's service in getting all of the essentials into the trunk of her Oldsmobile and then shepherding Liselotte down Highway 99.

Although I offered to rearrange my house with Liselotte's comfort in mind, she wouldn't hear of it, and she insisted on just sacking out on the sofa in the living room.

And so every evening, usually between nine and nine-thirty, we'd put some sheets and blankets on the sofa, pull the floor lamp close to it, and also bring over a chair from the dining room to serve as an improvised nightstand.

That was the easy part.

Dealing with Ramses, though, was something completely new for her. She'd never shared living space with a feline before.

At first she wasn't sure how to act around him. Look at him or not look? And, if she made eye contact with the Imperial One, how long should she stare at him? Let him approach or back away if he came too close? Another key concern: Should she pet him? If so, when, and how, exactly? On the top of his head, along his back?

Most disturbing for her was Ramses' uncouth behavior during our meals. When Liselotte and I were seated in the dining room with our plates in front of us and our silverware at the ready, he'd jump up onto the table and make some tentative, exploratory steps toward my plate or hers. If he chose to zero in on her food, she was at a loss. How should she act? If she shushed him away, would he get surly, or upset, or even strike out at her? Ramses' laser beam focus on her meal unsettled her, and invariably I'd reach over, grab him from behind, and unceremoniously plop him down on the floor before the standoff went on any longer.

Soon enough, however, they became fast friends. On many days, after I barreled off to school, Liselotte was constrained to stay inside to safeguard her eyes, and since she couldn't always read—especially right after the two major surgeries—she usually had to content herself with sitting on the sofa and immersing herself in classical music on KVPR. Ramses—with that distinct, enviable sensitivity that cats often manifest—stayed by her side, literally. Always, when I got back home later in the afternoon, the two of them were sitting next to each other, transfixed, focused on the radio's offerings—Ramses, true to form, in his elegant Sphinx pose.

Liselotte's eyes mended well—thanks in no small part to his presence and affectionate support.

# LORENZO

Before Nanda appeared in the summer of 1994, I'd spent several quality years with just Tribble. After that I got used to two cats on the premises. When Liselotte was well enough to resume her regular life back in Lodi, Ramses continued to be my sole cat companion for a while, but it was only a matter of time until that changed. Early in June 2008 I found myself checking out the cat center at the animal shelter once again. One reason: another multi-week trip I'd planned and paid for, and my concern that Rams shouldn't spend so much time inside a lonely house alone.

The tabby I zeroed in on had curious, roaming eyes, and before too long I pointed him out to one of the attendants, took care of the paperwork and payment for him, and chauffeured him back to the old homestead.

I was in for a rude surprise.

*My plan at the tail end of the school year was to find a kitten at the animal shelter, bring him home, and make sure that Ramses wouldn't be alone and lonely during my three-week sojourn overseas. All of that backfired when Ramses rejected Lorenzo completely and began staying outside more and more.*

I'd expected that past would be prologue and that this new pair would eventually become the same sort of BFFs that Tribble and Nanda had been for eons, or that Tribble and Falkor had grown into after a brief get–to–know–each–other period. Ditto for Falkor and Ramses: the pattern now seemed to be solid and dependable.

But these two would never really become a pair at all.

Ramses took an immediate and unremitting dislike to Lorenzo, one that didn't let up despite my promptings and deepest hopes. Instead of the bathtub—Tribble's sanctuary back in the day—Ramses located safe spaces outdoors and shunned the house more and more.

*At this point he's been living outside exclusively for about a week and a half. Not alone, apparently in the company of a few feline cronies, especially one gray and white one (maybe his lady love).*

Maybe a chemical fix would improve matters, I figured.

The pet store up the street offered a product with pheromones, something that you could plug into a power outlet. According to the blurb on the packaging, it would prompt cats to overcome negative emotions like anxiety or anger. It was worth a shot, but the gizmo was either defective or ineffective, or Ramses' repugnance was just too massive for treatments like this one.

In the following months Ramses took to spending so much time outside that Lorenzo became the de facto indoor cat and Rams the anywhere–but–indoor pet. I only spotted him a few times a week, usually out back. Sometimes, on languid summer evenings, I'd take a paperback outside and make myself comfortable underneath one of the fruit trees.

*From time to time I've been sitting outside on the lawn. reading something like <u>East of Eden</u> or <u>A Thousand Splendid Suns</u>, and he'd appear and position himself sphinx-like at a secure distance from me.*

My patience and occasional encouragement usually paid dividends. Ramses would monitor for me from a distance, then close the gap between us warily and then not so warily. More often than not he'd wind up spending some quality time, just–like–in–the–good–old–days quality time, nestled in my lap. At times I pressed my luck and tried to schlep him back into the house, but there he drew his line in the proverbial sand. Whenever I approached the back door with him in my arms, he fidgeted, protested, struggled mightily, and then broke away from me. The spell of reconciliation was rent asunder.

The date of my flight to Germany was fast approaching, which made Ramses's recalcitrance all the more troubling.

*His distance and attitude have affected me more than I would have expected—in part because of my false assumption that he would get along with Lorenzo, in part because of the other worries and anxieties pecking at me these days.*

All in all, I told myself, I'd arranged things as well as they possibly could be. Shannon Radbill, one of Marty's sons and a former student of mine, would be coming over every day when I was gone. He'd dole out food and water and TLC inside the house, then give Ramses double rations of food and water outside—once on the back steps, then again inside the garage, which he could access through a cat door.

*That way the moochers can eat some of the grub too, and that way he'll get the idea to spend some time inside the garage, away from the Fresno summer sun and local predators and marauders.*

Fortuna smiled on me that time. After I got back to Fresno later that summer, Ramses showed up in a few days, and regular Ramses sightings— as exciting and amazing as spotting UFOs —began happening again.

# KITTENS

A single cat, care of Lenny. Then a pair of them, thanks again to Lenny. But over time I've gotten to the point where, now in the 2020s, I'm saddled with five or six of them.

Things had started to change when a feral cat took a liking to the murky nooks in my garage and the cool, inviting niches in my backyard. A feral female. One that was pregnant.

Matters came to a head late in July 2009.

*Five kittens are now in control of my bedroom, along with their mom. I'm keeping them there until I can find them all a home. I got the kittens spayed/neutered earlier this week at The Cathouse by the Kings in Parlier. I put an ad in the* Bee *that will start running next Tuesday. I also made an appointment to have their mom, a feral cat that's been living in the garage and backyard for several months, spayed. I'm thinking of adopting her formally and naming her Faustina.*

Once the feisty black and white kitten escaped from my bedroom and I went after it, finally fishing it out of its hiding place behind the refrigerator. Another time, when I came in with their food, it looked at first as if they'd all managed to escape—and then it turned out that all of them were huddling in the space underneath the chest of drawers.

The new houseguests disrupted my carefully laid summer plans.

*Today, according to my original plan for these weeks, I would have driven up to Fort Bragg, then spent some days with Lenny, then moved on from there to meet with Peter and Terry in their retirement paradise in Bellingham. Now, if I'm lucky—if the cats find new owners, if the mom is spayed and she recovers well, if I can find someone to watch over the house—I might be able to get away in two weeks or so.*

Landing comfy homes for these animals was easier hoped for than accomplished.

*Today is the last day that my classified ad will run in the <u>Fresno Bee</u>. So far only two people have contacted me with an interest in the kittens, and none of the critters has found a home yet.*

The solution to this dilemma, at least for some of my new houseguests, turned out to be as plain as the welcome mat outside my front door.

*My plan at this point: on Thursday I'll bring Faustina to the animal hospital to be checked out. Faustina needs her sutures removed anyway, and she needs to be looked at if I'm going to care for her long-term. I'll also bring two of the kittens to the animal shelter on Thursday morning. The chance that they'll be put down remains, but Ramses couldn't abide with so many other felines in the garden, and the problem will only be exacerbated when they start growing up and getting even more assertive.*

The plan filled me with some misgivings. I'd hoped to find homes for all of them, and now it looked as if the best I could do was to adopt three kittens, along with the mom, and let fate and the animal shelter deal with the others.

*Before this May I had no idea of how extreme the problem of abandoned or feral felines was in this town; now it's one more theme that can weigh me down. The phone might yet ring; someone might still check out petfinders.com and contact me; but it seems likely that the day after tomorrow I'll step back into my pre–feral–kitten life and reclaim my bedroom. It'll be tough to gather the two black and white kittens into the cat carrier, and rough to drive them over to the animal shelter, but another alternative—paying for each of them so that they get room and board at the Cathouse—doesn't work either.*

# CYPRESS

Ramses was still outside, but hardly a hermit. In the middle of August I noticed him *wandering around the back garden with his gray and white consort.*

Around the same time I noticed *nervousness and ambivalence—and occasional fits of anger*—welling up inside, and I put these down in part to *Ramses and his ongoing estrangement from this house and from me.*

During some intervals he didn't appear at all, and I grew to accept my rare, sporadic interactions with him. I took it for granted that he'd appear now and then, especially since I set out food for him when he did show up, and I kept on nourishing the hope that he might eventually be reconciled with Lorenzo and the others inside.

For a few mornings in a row he abruptly materialized close to the back door, peering up at me with what looked like longing, even pleading. When I went out and approached him, though, he scrambled over the brick wall into the driveway and off to who knew where.

In 1990, when I bought the house and moved in, I tried out some house cleaners listed in the phone book. Many of them turned out to be overpriced and generally unsatisfactory. At last I came across Priscilla Fleming, a pleasant and industrious house cleaner who wound up tending to the place for years and years. Many times she'd drop by and clean everything while I was away at work, but not always. Once, when she was getting ready to leave, she let me know about a disturbing odor out by the flower bed along my driveway.

After she pulled away in her car, I went there and checked it out. Sure enough, there was a pungent stench close to the cypress along the southeast side of the house—the stink of something decaying. I spread aside the bottom branches and found Ramses' body there on the concrete.

I'd already read about this a few times—that cats, when they're in pain, seek out a solitary place, and they often wind up dying there. Over the last few days I'd searched for Ramses, of course, but I'd never thought to examine this particular spot.

I dug a grave for Ramses in what had now become the go-to cat burial site out back. Once again it was tough to reconcile the disconnect between this desiccated shape I was covering with dirt and the keen, attentive Ramses that held sway in my soul and memory.

# FAUSTINA

Some cats, far more than others, shine with a distinct personality, an aura, a strong presence. In my life one of those was Faustina, the pregnant feral cat that I wound up adopting.

In literature Faustina was the name that Johann Wolfgang Goethe gave to the beloved in his sultry *Roman Elegies*. In ancient history Faustina was the wife of Marcus Aurelius Antonius, the Roman emperor and stoic who penned the *Meditations*.

For me Faustina, in her feline incarnation, was first and foremost a lady—dignified, bright, and poised—and my memories of her always include her devoted but unlikely paramour, Scruffy—a wizened, street-smart survivor of a tomcat. He joined her after I'd formally adopted her, and they sure made an unusual couple. For all that, though, they were profoundly devoted to one another. When they lounged atop my trash containers in the backyard and gazed lovingly at each other, I was reminded above all of the Etruscan burial sculptures that I'd come across during my second visit to Rome in 2003:

Beyond the marvelous bond that connected them, there was a stateliness and grace to their movements that commanded my attention and admiration. Yes, even Scruffy shaped up and stayed on his best behavior in his consort's presence.

Faustina hardly felt confined to the likes of my modest garden. More often than not she was out and about, checking out other homes and green areas up and down the street. Once she missed morning feeding time. Soon afterwards, when I went out to the front to water the flower beds, she appeared on the south side of the street, power walking straight towards me. I scolded her for being late for her breakfast, but, given her aristocratic outlook on everything, she took my admonitions in stride.

Scruffy was a rough-and-tumble street tough, the dour survivor of sundry rumbles and violent encounters, but for all that his eyes held nothing but affection and adoration for his beloved. He was far older than Faustina, and one spring morning, before zipping off to Edison High, I found his lifeless body on my driveway, curled underneath the water meter of the neighbor's house. By all appearances he'd died a gentle and painless death.

I took a few moments to put his limp body into the compost bin and cover him up with some grass cuttings that the gardener had dumped in there earlier. There he was concealed and safe until I could honor his passing. Later on, after the end of the school day, I found the time and the frame of mind to bury him.

If Faustina suffered from that loss, she never betrayed it. Her wide-ranging perambulations continued unabated, as did her regular intervals of evening repose atop one of the trash containers.

Faustina herself perished about a year later.

At first I didn't even register what had happened. Stepping out front to grab the morning paper, I spied her close to the curb, apparently sunning herself on the strip of lawn next to my driveway. It was only later on, when I approached her, that I noticed that she wasn't reacting to me at all. When I touched her, she was stiff and unresponsive. Rigor mortis had already started to set in and spread.

Apparently a car had run her over on the normally placid street that fronts my property. After she was hit, someone else—probably a neighbor, though I've never found out which one—brought her body over to the front of my house and left her there for me to find, and maybe to prevent her from being run over again by someone else.

Shock hits you, then it subsides a little…and then activity helps you to deal with the blow. I prepared another grave out back in the now-traditional location. When I found Falkor's skull still in the dirt down there, I set it aside, and when I laid Faustina down in the hole I'd regardfully made for her, I placed his skull between her front paws so that she was fondling it, or caressing it, or taking care of it in a fervent, regal way. It seemed fitting not to leave her alone, but in the company of one of her dear companions.

# Max And Moritz

Faustina might have passed, but her offspring were still very much a part of my household and my soul.

For example, the black one and the white one.

I named them Max and Moritz, a reference to the pair of rascals in the series of Wilhelm Busch poems that first appeared in 1865.

They were never as outlandish as their namesakes, but they definitely turned out to share some traits with that literary pair.

In Busch's poems and the unforgettable drawings that accompany them the two boys carry out a series of sly pranks, some of them gruesome and even downright cruel. In their first adventure they devise a way of killing a widow's chickens by connecting the birds' food with string. When the animals swallow their food as well as much of the string, they struggle to fly away, only to wind up panicking and inadvertently killing themselves off.

In a later section Max and Moritz conspire against one of their teachers. They sneak into his house and, knowing his weakness for smoking his pipe, substitute gunpowder for tobacco. When the pedagogue settles down for the evening a few hours later on and, true to his ingrained habit, lights up his pipe, the results are immediate and catastrophic. Although the teacher survives, he's lost his hair and his skin has turned black.

My two critters, though rambunctious, certainly didn't take things to such extremes. I soon found out, though, that I couldn't plant vegetables from seed in the garden anymore. Once, when I put in some seeds for bush beans along the eastern fence, both of them became fascinated by the loose soil that now graced that spot, and it became their favorite venue for outdoor wrestling. That summer they were so full of beans that I almost wound up not harvesting any beans of my own.

When I got home during the school year, usually in mid-afternoon, actually getting into my house wasn't a straightforward matter. I couldn't just unlock the back door and bring my teacher gear inside. The crew of cats—Max and Moritz front and center among them—were lying in wait for me, each insisting on some serious petting time.

After I emerged from the garage, they were all on the back lawn as a sort of eager welcoming committee. Once I petted a cat, he'd swing around and take up a position closer to the door, so that before I could get inside, I wound up meeting and greeting almost every one of them at least twice. Soon enough Max, the White Wonder, landed on a variation of the no-frills greeting committee scenario. When I made my appearance, he'd dash back toward the apricot tree in the center of the yard, then scamper up the trunk and along one of the lower branches. My task in this game—and, with time, it became a regular and unavoidable game—was to reach up and pet him, although petting Max was no simple five- or ten-second routine, but something that involved a full facial massage plus much, much more.

Max's relentless need to get my attention was something that I'd never encountered before. He often insisted on slipping into the house, and once indoors he typically wound up close to me, wherever that was—on the desk in the study, on the table next to the computer tower, or flopped down on the living room sofa, looking at me expectantly and lovingly.

There's an old saw about how challenging it can be to herd cats. Forget about it. Just getting a single one to pose for a simple portrait can be exasperating beyond words.

One Friday afternoon my intention was as simple as sunlight. Max always relished the chance to sneak inside the house and then take his privileged place on top of the sofa—so why not let him do just that and then snap a picture of him in all of his spunky glory?

My plan was straightforward, clear-cut. Executing it turned out to be daunting.

On typical days Max would leap up onto the sofa and find his special spot, usually a place off to the northernmost side, and then hunker down for an hour or two, give or take. This time things were different, though, probably because I was brandishing a camera and watching him, lavishing attention on him that flattered and intrigued him—and prompted a set of agitated, restless maneuvers.

For a while he paced around the sofa as if stalking something…

…or he'd lean over the edge to peer down at the floor, rapt with attention at who knew what.

Try as I might, getting a shot that matched my aesthetic aspirations as well as his typical relaxed and mellow indoor behavior just wouldn't work out. Max would bend curiously toward my camera…

...or his movements became so quick and unpredictable that I couldn't even capture his full glory inside the frame:

Max vanished one day and never showed his face again, but his spirit still haunts this place, alongside those of many of his compatriots.

# Momo

She's a thoughtful girl, wise beyond her years, and she's the title character of Michael Ende's novel *Momo*. Her special trait and amazing power: she can solve your problems. How? Just by listening to you, by immersing herself in what you're telling her. Her seamless attention helps you to vanquish your troubles on your own.

As Ende tells it, when foolish people speak with Momo, they get clever ideas. Those who are clueless and undecided suddenly figure out what they need to do. Some see their lives as being meaningless. When they meet Momo, though, the truth hits them: they're important for the world just as they are.

And so I figured that "Momo" would be a good fit for the female kitten that I'd adopted from Faustina's brood.

So far all the names that I'd chosen had been spot-on in the long run. This time, however...not that much.

This time there's been a lingering disconnect between the Momo of Ende's fantasy novel and the feline Momo poking around out back. It wouldn't work out as it had with Tribble, who—at least in his youthful, pre-portly days—embodied all the cutes and cuddliness of his Trekkie brethren.

Momo the cat lacks all focussed, well-honed listening skills. Quite the opposite: she's skittish and evasive, uneasy when she finds herself too close to others. If I hear her plaintive meowing in the front and step outside to track her down, she'll start to prance away, usually toward the neighbor's lawn, complaining the whole time about my proximity and my rudeness.

She isn't the sort to seek and maintain eye contact or encourage physical contact of any sort with me or anyone else. She cherishes her independence and her distance, and she's openly nervous when I come too close to her. I'm guessing that she meows out front just to make sure that I'm home, that I'm close at hand and, by extension, that I'll be divvying up food again later in the day. Beyond that, she wants little to do with me. She also tends to stay away from the other felines. She prefers her private, clandestine haunts inside the garage or underneath the rosebushes to open, observable spots on the lawn.

If she doesn't solve problems and resolve issues like her namesake, though, she seldom causes any problems on her own.

Of course, a nanoproblem arises now and then when her curiosity trumps her skittishness. Sometimes, when I leave the back door ajar, she'll sneak inside and start to explore each room in turn. When I get back in and shut the door, she panics, and she finds herself facing a thorny dilemma. Does she come back toward the door—where I am? Or does she locate a secure place somewhere inside? Her anguished cries help me to figure out where she is, and once I spot her, I can herd her—sort of—back outside. Before she takes her leave, she spends some time performing a set of artful stretches on the doormat, then scratches at it vehemently for good measure. Then, when she's good and ready, she bolts down the steps and out of sight.

# Stopping Time

After a while you figure out a system. If something happens, or if something doesn't happen the way you expect, you know what to do.

Once, late in 2018, Lorenzo didn't show up for his morning meal, and I did what came automatically. I searched around the whole backyard, checking underneath the sprawling rosebushes and then behind them. I took my time going through the garage, and I made sure that he wasn't up in the storage space close to the rafters.

I went out into the back alley, reconnoitered that stretch, and crossed that possibility off my list.

At last I went around the whole perimeter of the house. I found Lorenzo's body lying on my neighbor's driveway.

Apparently, from what I could piece together later, a feral dog had come upon him during the night and cornered him there. His eyes, still open, were full of defiance. He hadn't gone down without a frenzied fight.

A set of habits, a procedure that you've developed and that you find yourself following. I brought a plastic sheet outside and laid him on top of it, then carried him into the backyard, where I prepared his grave. My sister Barbara was staying with me during that time. She was a late sleeper, but at nine or so I knocked on her door, let her rub residual sleep out of her eyes, and gave her the news.

It's a routine, and you complete each step the way you've done it before, but it's never quite the same. Especially important is the moment after you've finished the grave and laid your friend down into it. It's when you stop time and let silence offer its benediction, when thoughts about the one you lost give way to inchoate feelings. You honor the time that you spent with someone by pausing time for a while, by allowing a space for other things—wonder, gratitude, a choking sense of absence.

When it came to Lorenzo, that interlude needed to be long and substantial.

# OLIVER

In the days that followed there was a palpable gap in the household, and after a few weeks it became clear that we needed to fill it with a new pet. Not another Lorenzo, of course. Lorenzo de Medici, his namesake, had flown high in the world of Florentine banking in the fifteenth century. My Lorenzo had also been one of a kind, a fat cat to be reckoned with and never to be equaled. Still, Gulliver, his sidekick, needed a new companion, and so one Saturday morning I headed over to the animal shelter and adoption center again. Barbara tagged along; after all, she had a stake in who would be moving in.

As it turned out, the calendar year was coming to an end, and the week that we'd chosen featured a special "Adopt a Cat" discount rate—all the more impetus to take our search earnestly. Still, none of the cats we first spotted stood out as likely candidates, and it was beginning to look as if this expedition would end in failure. Things seemed brighter when we picked out a few finalist cats, and they looked even better when the shelter staff let us give each of them a "hold" test. A staff member brought out each finalist, one by one, so that we could take turns holding it in our arms and checking out how it literally felt—to see if a bond could exist, or if it already did.

Soon enough we came up with our winner—yet another tabby.

Christening the new one proved to be easier than expected, especially when Barbara and I put our heads together and tossed around a gaggle of possibilities. We definitely needed a name that honored Lorenzo's memory, and at the same time we needed something that would show his connection to Gulliver—one that we hoped would take root and flourish over time. Then—presto. Oliver rhymes—sort of, more or less—with Gulliver. More to the point, the first two initials—O and L—were the reverse of L and O, the start of Lorenzo's name. And this time around our choice was another prescient one.

In a way. To some extent.

In their day Tribble and Lorenzo had been voracious and gluttonous, but with time Oliver came to give them both a run for their money.

Not satisfied with the portion he's received at the parish workhouse, the central figure in Charles Dickens's *Oliver Twist* approaches the master and says, famously, "'Please, sir, I want some more.'" In the early days our Oliver would likewise make civil, polite requests for seconds. He'd fervently make eye contact along with gentle purring noises, then keep that up for a while. If that didn't get him the goods—and it never did—he'd sprawl out on the linoleum floor and remind us, in case it had somehow slipped our minds, just how cute and delightful he could look. When that stunt didn't do the trick, he was plainly at a loss, perplexed and stumped.

Over time the less than successful "Look at me, I'm adorable" phase faded. Before long he was pining, then demanding, then protesting and shrieking with full-throated venom.

So maybe "Oliver" hasn't been an entirely good fit for this one after all. "'A little more'" is hardly this guy's definition of a square deal.

Fade into an afternoon scene not that long ago. Oliver's still hungry and he's still on the prowl, with edibles on his mind and in his crosshairs. I find him squatting on my kitchen counter and leaning over the sink, where a Tower of Pisa stack of unwashed plates awaits attention, and he's busying himself with licking at whatever remnants of pasta or veggies or veggie patties are glued to the top plate. He's so intent on his project that he barely registers my approach.

Oliver, it turns out, isn't a cat as much he is a mouth—a voracious, ever desperate orifice in search of sustenance, even if it's the stuck–on–a–plate–that–urgently–needs–to–be–cleaned type of nourishment. His violent hunger doesn't discriminate and it doesn't reject. As he ferrets out scraps to satisfy his endless appetite, he's the soul of tolerance and acceptance. If it's in the kitchen, it's by definition acceptable and edible.

Once he's launched into his eating cycle, he'll suffer no disturbances at all. Once I tried to spoon a little extra into his bowl at that point, but he just batted the spoon away from me in a fury. Clearly I had no understanding of his needs and his priorities.

# Gulliver

Sometimes new cats just turn up out of nowhere. It's as if a portal from another dimension has materialized, and out they step.

One summer evening in 2010 I heard an awful racket coming from out back. An incredibly tiny, frightened tabby was lying in the middle of the yard—tense, anxious, bawling, and, as I soon determined, famished. I brought him inside, set out a bowl for him—and a new soul mate had arrived on the scene.

Where he came from remains unclear. It could be that someone with kittens, anxious to just get rid of them somehow, went down the back alley and tossed them here and there into random yards. Or maybe this kitten somehow got separated from his siblings and mother and couldn't find his way back to them.

Once his trauma subsided and he got used to hanging out in my place, he took to inspecting the bookcases in the living room. Time and time again he singled out one specific paperback on the bottom shelf—Jonathan Swift's *Gulliver's Travels*—and pawed at it until it tumbled onto the floor. This way, I imagined, he was trying to let me know that his name was Gulliver, and that he wanted me to address him that way. Only years later did it cross my mind that, actually, his true name might be Jonathan, and that I'd misconstrued his message. By that time, of course, it was much too late. By then his handle was definitely Gulliver, and, given the way that he explores the neighborhood—boldly, with unflagging resolve—the name works well for him.

Something similar, of course, had happened in the eighties when Tribble first came into my apartment in southeast Fresno. At that time a German *Reclam* paperback of Schopenhauer's writings had caught the black cat's eye and paw, and his obsession inspired a last name of sorts for him.

These two incidents are anomalous, though. None of the other felines has ever exhibited much curiosity about the rows and rows of book things around here. Oliver, of late, has taken to napping on my pile of recent *Economists* and *New Yorkers*, but that's about it.

Not all cats are picky about what they eat, and most of mine have been content when, after what for them was an interminable wait, I finally see fit to set munchies down in front of them. But Gulliver has proved to be very much the exception to that rule.

When it comes to being choosy, he takes the cake—although, judging from his habits, he'd probably reject several cakes before landing on the one that meets his standards. After all of this time he still sometimes catches me off guard with the sheer extent of his fickleness about his meals.

Feeding him, especially in the evening, I'm like a waiter in a fine restaurant. It's as if I'm opening a bottle of wine for a discriminating diner; as he takes a sip and then announces his judgement of its merits or egregious shortcomings, I remain silent and dutiful. In reality I'm pulling open a can of the wet food—one of the salmon cans, or another one labeled chicken something—and leaning down and letting him sniff at it. If his eyes turn eager and he starts heading toward the bowl, that's a promising sign, but hardly a sure thing. Many evenings I've spooned out a chunk from a can like that, but when he approaches, he takes one or two tentative licks only to back off decisively.

Nor will he leave it there, with the act of rejection. He'll stalk me around the house until—hey, this is Gulliver, my longtime homey—I follow him into the kitchen a second time to try out another kitty entrée.

His abject capriciousness is exacerbating. You'd figure that he'd always go for the seafood choice or the chicken, but you'd be wrong. His tastes are fickle, they change, and when it comes to his dinner predilections past is hardly ever prologue. Sometimes it turns out that I've actually served up the right meal this time, but he insists that I turn his bowl around 180 degrees, and only then will he deign to lick at its contents. Another variation on that theme: I plunk the same food into another bowl, and now he puts it all away in a flash.

Nowadays I usually bring him into the bedroom to serve him his food on my bedspread. That's become a sensible routine because of some tooth extractions he needed last year, procedures that put the brakes on his masticating efficiency. At first, of course, I naively tried to feed some cats together in the kitchen, but no dice. After making quick work of his own serving, Oliver would rush over to his brother's dish and attack it with relish and feverish abandon. His favored tactic was as primitive as it was efficacious. He bit into a hefty chunk of Gulliver's meal, then dumped it onto the kitchen floor and scarfed it down with mindless speed, as if he were the longstanding champion in some high-stakes hot dog eating contest.

To avoid these sorts of mealtime calamities I now set out Oliver's food first. Then, while the joy of eating distracts him, I put Gulliver's wet food into a dish, pick him up with my right hand while holding onto his dish with my left, and give him a ride worthy of a Disneyland theme park back to my bedroom. When I get to the door, he invariably grows antsy and restless. He begins to struggle against my hold, something that's precipitated unfortunate food accidents—e.g., the food plummeting to the hardwood floor. Not that that stops him from finishing it all off, of course.

Tribble's trademark and forte was his robust face push, and Gulliver has a similar attribute. When I'm lying down somewhere—on the sofa, on my bed—he'll leap up beside me and look me over. Then, when the moment seems auspicious to him, he tentatively begins to climb up onto my stomach, gazing at me intently all the while. He edges ever closer toward my face, then starts licking it systematically. When I reach up and massage him around his mouth and neck, he's in heaven. He closes his eyes halfway in delight; his head sways from side to side.

Sometimes this business seems genuine and innocent: he just craves my attention for its own sake. Other times, though, he definitely aims to get some more food out of me. This becomes obvious when, at some point, I start to get up, and he clambers onto the floor, ready and eager to guide me back toward the kitchen and the culinary delights that are waiting there.

# Maxwell

Sometimes cats come along and finagle their way into your life. A new one will begin to make an appearance in the backyard, often just observing the goings-on from afar. The ones that have already established their squatting rights there will initially greet the newbie with indifference or even disdain. The latter will become especially pronounced should the newcomer edge closer toward the back door—in particular if it's close to mealtime. Typically the old-timers will take turns closing in on the newbie and chasing him over the fence. This initial stage might last a few weeks, and I imagine that the guys take their cue from me. If they see me accepting this fresh face—say, by offering it food—then they'll follow suit and fall into line.

Such was the case a few years ago with Maxwell.

I first noticed him when he was doing his spying–on–all–of–us–from–afar routine. He sat, as sphinxlike as a Ramses wannabe, behind the semidwarf peach tree and watched some of the regulars mingling by the trash containers, or lounging on top of some of them. His intent observation, relentless and penetrating, led me to call him Maxwell, a nod to the nineteenth-century Scottish scientist who made significant contributions to electromagnetic theory. At the same time, of course, "Maxwell" was close to "Max," who'd been Moritz's brother and who vanished, mysteriously, a few years ago.

Soon enough, though, the name fit for a very different reason. As Maxwell monitored his subjects' actions from his post behind the peach tree, he seemed to think he was invisible—and of course he was anything but. The same thing happened on other occasions. When I was watering the vegetables, he'd stay put and observe me steadily. If I turned and looked in his direction, he'd dash behind a rosebush or a tree, apparently believing he'd outwitted me and kept his presence under wraps. His comical antics made me think of Maxwell Smart, the hapless secret agent in the sixties TV series *Get Smart.*

Once I began feeding him, the others started, begrudgingly at first, to accept his newfound status. Even then, though, he often stayed away from them during mealtimes—maybe out of respect or circumspection, or maybe because he felt intimidated.

His feeding habits were, and continue to be, downright perplexing. When I come toward him with his food, he turns away from me and even takes a few preliminary steps toward the back gate. It's as if I have to woo him, to coax him to look over at his food and sidle up to it. The procedure's a gradual one, and it can't be rushed. At long last he drops his head down into his bowl and starts licking his meal slowly. Then he incrementally settles down on the grass until he's lying on his stomach. Now he's reached his ideal dining pose, and at last he can devote himself wholeheartedly to pecking at his chow.

# JOHANN

At first, he was very much an interloper of the Scruffy mold. A food bandit, he lurked close by at mealtimes. He was cunning and sly, and experience had made him as deft as a master pickpocket. Without warning he'd pounce on other cats' bowls, lift chunks out whole, plop them down on the lawn and dig into them with voracious abandon. Then he'd scram, and he'd stay out of sight until his next foray. Even when he stayed longer—and I began setting out his very own bowl—he shunned attention and, especially, physical contact. Touching him or petting him in any way was off-limits. His very reluctance goaded me to try to win his favor and his trust.

Achieving that objective took weeks. I started petting him—just a bit—while he was busy eating, something he grew to tolerate. Physical contact at any other time continued to be off-limits and risky.

Then, one day, there was a great leap forward. I came across him out on the lawn. He spied me in the act of spying him and rolled on his side, offering his belly for me to stroke.

An even bigger breakthrough happened after he got into a vicious fight with a neighborhood adversary. The injuries he sustained on his neck and face were so severe that he needed (a) to get extensive treatment at the animal hospital, and (b) to stay inside, with an E-collar around his neck, for a week and a half. To say he was stir-crazy during that time would be understating things considerably. If he wasn't literally climbing the walls, that was just because he was still in recuperation mode.

I regularly joined him in the room I'd set aside for him and brought along reading material so that my visits could last longer. Back then I was working my way through the final volumes of Len Deighton's Bernie Samson series, and Johann got comfortable next to me as I sat in a virtual lotus position and devoured the paperbacks. Given how placid and relaxed he seemed, I imagined that he was enjoying Deighton's byzantine plots as much as I was.

# Muzio

is what I named a stray who showed up on my front doorstep one morning and just plain refused to go away for a while. He was a tiny fellow, but he roared with an insistent energy and a vim that few could resist. Certainly I couldn't.

Soon enough I was bringing out food for him like clockwork, and he showed me his appreciation by downing it all in record time. When he failed to vanish during the non-feeding hours—something I'd come to expect, given my experience with other cats—I set up a makeshift home for him next to the front door. Actually, it was nothing more than a cardboard box with some old blankets piled inside that acted as provisional bedding.

It turned out that Muzio's daily—and noisy—presence entranced and puzzled the mail carrier as she made her rounds. One afternoon she rang the doorbell and asked me about him. I could only tell her what I knew, which was close to zilch—that he was a gray, cantankerous stray, tiny but feisty, and that he'd singled out my digs to be his own.

When he first started bellowing querulously out front, I was working my way through some of Clementi's Opus 36 Piano Sonatinas. The composer's first name, I saw on the score, was Muzio, and so I came to associate those pieces with his antics.

Then, a few weeks later, he disappeared. Maybe one of the neighbors phoned Animal Control—after all, sometimes he'd been a loudmouth for hours on end—or maybe he just opted, for whatever inscrutable reason, to take his leave. After waiting a few days longer just in case he returned, I dismantled his bed.

# Nameless

Some of the cats that came around never got names—I never got to know them much. Unexpected but welcome, they dropped by for a time and then lingered in memory. Here's one example from my journal—a slice of time from the early 2000s in the Ramses-Falkor era:

*Yesterday morning I saw that the kitten owned by the renters next door had wandered over to my back porch and was drinking from the water bowl. Falkor seemed to accept her presence and her amiable curiosity. Later, also in the morning, I saw Ramses outside on the lawn, under the orange tree. The kitten was close by, watching him attentively as he rolled around on the grass and then playfully started "fighting" with her, repeating the routine a few times. These days are graced with small wonders.*

# BEER RUN

As the sole German instructor at both a high school and a middle school, I was responsible for a broad spectrum of courses—a lot broader than the two or three preps that most of my colleagues enjoyed—and so my evenings were typically loaded with hours of preparation. Of course, I'm not complaining. Both English and German were my passions, and I relished the opportunities afforded to me to fashion courses according to my students' needs and my strengths.

Still, the sheer number of classes to prepare for led to long stretches of prep time—and also the need, now and again, to take a break at about nine in the evening to go on a beer run before getting back to the final stretch of the day's workload. Down the street from my house there's a modest shopping plaza that's held, as its unofficial anchor for many a year, a liquor store—my mecca for many a nocturnal jaunt. The sanguine clerk behind the counter knew me well, and early on he got to know my predilections regarding suds. For a long while it would always be a six-pack of Dos Equis, or Sierra Nevada, or something from our local Sequoia Brewing Company. Now and then I'd venture into offbeat beer territory, but only rarely.

The route back home took five minutes at most, unless a dilatory red light at the intersection kept me waiting. Even so, I rarely had to take that walk alone. As soon as I crossed over Blackstone and got back into a realm of residential lawns and bungalows, the tapping of paws began to make themselves heard. Before I knew it, I had a squadron of my felines trailing behind me in formation. Sometimes I even imagined that we weren't just pedestrians on a suburban street at all. No way—we actually were a squadron, an elite group of planes on a clandestine mission, shooting over enemy territory and now heading back to our base, with me in the lead as its commander.

When we got to my front lawn, the cats would disperse into the semidarkness. I'd fish my keys out of my pocket and get back into the solace of my clean, well-lighted place—thankful for and also heartened by their company.

That's how things often played out, and how they always should have played out.

Sometimes my intended beer run had to be aborted, though. No beer, even when I was desperate for some—and even when my workload definitely merited a few bottles.

I'd get out of the house, start heading up the sidewalk—and then the cats would begin confronting me, whining and bickering. Were they anxious that I was leaving them, never to come back? Was this some kind of separation anxiety? Ignoring their antics and going toward my liquor store mecca wasn't without risks. I didn't want them chasing after me when I crossed a main thoroughfare. There were those evenings when I fired up the Acura and drove somewhere to get my fix, and other times, truth be told, when I reluctantly turned on my heel and headed back home, beerless but free of anxieties about the rest of my squadron.

# CIRCLE

Many times, more often than in the past, I've found myself leaning down toward some of the cats, especially Gulliver and Moritz of late, nuzzling and petting them, and then letting them know that I love them. But that never happened in the early years when Tribble was my sole housemate.

Why is that? Why do I feel closer to all of them now as opposed to a few decades ago? In part it's because I'm more aware of my own mortality, the blunt fact that my own life has an expiration date. Part ties in with the special cats that I've lost and the others that I'm sure to lose in time. In the back of my mind I know, when it comes to the older ones like Gulliver, that they'll pass one way or another over the next few years. And part of it stems from the COVID-inspired stay-at-home period. As trips and face-to-face encounters with other people dwindled for a time, the stature and status of these cats expanded.

In truth, though, they've always played a key role for me. I was just slow to pick up on that.

Take a sheet of paper, one that's completely blank. Draw a circle in the middle and write your name inside it. Here's what you do next:

Put together the planetary system that is you. Draw the other "planets"—the people who play important roles in your life. Those who are closer to the center—that circle with your name inside—will be in larger circles. Others, the less important souls, will find their places farther away, and they'll usually be in smaller circles. As you keep sketching, you'll draw and label some "planets" above your own, while others will appear alongside you or far beneath you.

Complete this sketch of your self, making sure to include all the people who contribute to who and what you are. When you're done, set it aside. File it away. Try not to think about it at all.

Then, a year or two later on, take out some more paper and make that sketch again. Put together another map of you. Don't think about it too much. Don't dawdle. Don't wonder why you've placed someone in a certain quadrant, or why you're giving one person a hefty circle and someone else a smallish one. Above all, don't peek—don't look at that earlier drawing of yours first.

I don't even remember where I first came across this idea, but it stuck with me, and for years my filing cabinet had a manila folder with a burgeoning set of "planetary systems" that showed my self over time. Interesting is how some things have shifted during the years and how others have stayed fairly constant. Sometimes people whom I drew bigger, and closer to me, have been replaced by others who came into my life later on—and who played the same role for me as those who preceded them in that spot.

It turns out, though, that all of those sketches were flawed. I'd only drawn and labeled circles of people. Quite a bit of that space, especially over the last thirty-odd years, should have featured cats as well as dogs, my own pets as well as the animal cohorts in my friends' houses.

How I missed that for so long baffles me.

# GARDEN

Most buildings look substantial and even imperishable. Stand next to them and you have the sense that they've got a firm hold on that spot, that they'll stay put and stay intact and constant for eons to come.

Those who dwell inside know better. They've seen how this building and its surroundings shift over time.

Introducing cats into an area can trigger those sorts of mutations. All of a sudden the space isn't quite the same. Some places inside and out begin to change, and it goes on and on as long as the cats are around.

Start with the garden, especially the one out back. Exhibit A harkens back to my high school days.

It stood a few feet in front of me and commanded my attention during my first two years of German at Lodi High.

It was my teacher's lectern, and it took a prominent place in front of us in our classroom, flanked by an array of eye-catching German-themed wall posters.

Otto Linberger—The Big Cheese, as we affectionately nicknamed him—conducted most of his lessons from behind that podium stand, and those moments stayed with me long after I graduated from the home of the Lodi Flames.

Decades later I dropped by the school to visit with him. He'd been moved to a new classroom—a lowly portable, mundane but serviceable—and the old lectern was still there, still with him.

And then he let me know that he'd be retiring in a few months and that his lectern would soon be homeless.

I prevailed upon him to let me have it. There wasn't a comparable lectern in my classroom down in Fresno, and I'd put his to good use. Think of it, Otto, I told him—the tradition would continue. This was something that belonged in a German classroom, and it would continue in that role for many years to come.

Otto concurred, and he came up with an easy way for me to get it from him. He had a connection with some business people in Fresno, and they'd bring it to their office down there and hold it for me.

One balmy afternoon I drove the Dasher over to an industrial park close to where Ashlan Avenue crosses over Highway 99. The receptionist behind the counter was immersed in some online video game, and when I introduced myself and told her what I wanted, she just snorted, "Oh, *that* thing." Then she led me into an adjacent storage room and waved at the object of my quest.

I brought my trophy outside with care and caution, fed it into the hatchback, and headed on home.

Then I wound up never taking it into my classroom at all.

The vision of standing behind Otto Linberger's lectern and teaching German was thrilling, compelling. Realistically, though, my room was already too crowded with desks and worktables as it was. The dream was tantalizing, but—when I took some measurements and looked at everything practically—there was just no way to squeeze this thing into the front of the room so that all of the students would have a clear view of it.

So…what to do with my prize, Otto Linberger's totem? As a temporary measure I set it into the flower bed behind the garage. Temporary stretched into more than that when, somehow, it began to look and feel natural there. It eventually became a permanent fixture, and there it stands even now.

The felines have all come to adore it. The slanted top especially appeals to them. The place that once held Otto's German textbook is now where they sun themselves on warm afternoons. In their eyes the whole thing, now a hulk of sun-battered wood, is probably just one mammoth and delightful scratching post.

Moritz is especially enamored of it. His hard-core routine with me, of course, is the one that he inherited from Max. When he spies me approaching, he typically races toward the base of the apricot tree, scratches at its bark vigorously, then bounds up the trunk and along one of the lower branches, where he takes a breather and gazes back at me expectantly. My task, of course, is to reach up and pet him, at which point he ambles along the branch and hops onto another one, then another, so that our petting sessions need to be reprised multiple times.

In the past few years, though, Moritz has alternated his frenzied dashes to the apricot tree with sprints targeting this new objective, the top of Otto's now decrepit and weather-beaten lectern. Once there, he looks over at me, challenging if not even commanding me to approach, and of course he expects me to devote some time and no small effort to giving him quality TLC. Breaking off either of these encounters—the apricot tree, the lectern—is a delicate process, one that would challenge the most seasoned of diplomats. When I stop giving him the strokes he feels he's entitled to, his paw goes after me with increasing insistence and even viciousness.

The lectern, the apricot tree…and then, of course, there's the hangout which Falkor and Ramses used to frequent during oven-hot summers.

*Falkor and Ramses have both taken to spending their afternoons under the cover of the greenery below my bathroom and bedroom windows. When I call them in for their din-din, they leap out from the plants, shake themselves so hard that their collars tinkle, and do their ritual stretches. A few days ago Ramses didn't come out right away. I bent down in front of the stretch of green and saw his face framed by branches and leaves.*

Not everything has always been placid and idyllic out there, of course. Being under the cats' purview, the backyard also became a place to hunt, to assail, and to kill without mercy.

It's May in 2021, and bad feelings are simmering out there. A California scrub-jay is perched on a low branch of the pluot tree. He's looming over the cats down in the flower beds, and he's screeching bloody murder.

Past experience has taught me that one of my felines has probably assaulted and disposed of one of this bird's compatriots. Oliver and Moritz are the ones that it especially has in its sights, and they don't just feign indifference and apathy vis-à-vis its virulent cries; they actually seem to be oblivious to its rage. Sometimes, when one of them saunters across the lawn, the bird swoops down over it, like one of the malicious beasties in the classic Hitchcock film, and squawks to show its repugnance. Sometimes it actually comes in for a landing on the grass one or two feet from one of them, maybe trying to rattle this predator's conscience. No such luck, though. It's a balmy afternoon, a faint breeze livens up the otherwise sullen air, and the cats don't even seem to notice its livid anger at all.

So which one was it? Was Moritz the culprit this time around, or was it Oliver? Checking out the bird's actions and the behavior of these two suspects, I'd put my money on Oliver. It's hard to say why, exactly, but he's even more studiously indifferent to the bird's yammering than Moritz is, and that, in my book, points to his guilt.

And then there are the pigeons.

Now and again pigeons alight on my back lawn and stroll to and fro, oblivious to the mortal danger that lurks for them oh so close by. I don't have to see them myself to know that they're there. The cats' movements have changed, and the look in their eyes now betrays a concentrated interest in one specific site. After staking out a place on the lawn to watch their intended prey, they can inch toward their targets with gradual and deft precision—and still the pigeons, like happy-go-lucky tourists on the first day of their sojourn in a new city, have no clue. John Watson had a better grasp of what was going on in Conan Doyle's stories than these sorry birds ever did.

If being fit were truly needed to survive, you wonder why these creatures didn't ride off into evolution's sunset long, long ago.

# House

The changes that cats beget aren't limited to the garden. Once you let them into your home, they do their own brand of atmospheric interior decoration.

On a very elemental level you need to be mindful when they're in the area. No longer can you move around mechanically, and that's doubly true if the lights are dim or shut off. One of them might be lying comfortably—and, for you, invisibly—right in the middle of a hallway, and stepping into it or on top of it is best avoided for both parties. Ditto for when it comes to getting comfortable in a chair or on the sofa. Although everyone in the clan has his or her favorite spot, these can change over time, and later on, for some reason, the cats all start to hang out in new and wholly unexpected places.

You learn—and then forget, and then learn once again—to shut the storage closets. The one in the hallway features several shelves of towels and blankets, and if the door's ajar, that's like a flashing VACANCY sign at a highway motel for the felines. An open door means that, in short order, one or more will take up residence on a comfy pastel pile, and his drowsy eyes and laid-back body language are the same as a DO NOT DISTURB sign dangling from the knob of a hotel door.

The same goes for the laundry basket: I can't just robotically lift it up and bring it to the washing machine. Someone's liable to be lying inside, comfortably spreadeagled among the waves of shirts and pants.

Another target of cat shenanigans: the bathroom. Here Falkor was often the culprit, as I journaled back in November 1998:

*Falkor's new joy in life is making confetti out of any toilet paper rolls he can find.*

Nor has my desktop remained sacrosanct, as I noted back in 2002.

*Trib used to lie atop the desk in the study, always insinuating himself more and more into my area of the desk—a tactic he's also used on the bed.*

The kitchen offers even more opportunities for cat mischief. When I'm cooking at the stove, it's important to remain vigilant and never turn my back. Otherwise one of the troop might well leap up onto the counter and start licking at the saucepan's contents.

In a way, of course, you could see this as a compliment: they sure seem to appreciate my cooking.

Over the years most of the cats have targeted these and similar places, but the screen door at the front entrance is another matter entirely. That was always Lorenzo's exclusive domain.

It seemed that whenever he had the opportunity—whenever the screen door was in sight—Lorenzo would begin climbing right up its length, scaling his own private version of El Capitan. Never mind that, once he reached the top of the door frame, he'd be stuck and would need someone else's help to get him down from the screen. Sometimes I wasn't aware of his plight for a while, and he literally needed to hang on for a while until I found him there and brought him back down to Planet Earth. More than one visitor to my front door has been startled and nonplussed by the sight of a hefty tabby working his way up that screen mesh. It could be that the other cats, witnessing the fine mess that Lorenzo always got himself into, learned from his example and opted to find other, less daunting challenges for themselves.

For years an old upright piano stood in my living room. It was the one that my siblings and I had grown up with back in Lodi, and the cats always gave it a collective cold shoulder.

That changed in late 2019, when a seasoned piano tuner came over to work on it. As he wrapped up his labors, he showed me just how pathetic its innards were. Its best days and sounds were definitely long gone.

One morning, when I was driving up Fresno Street, I spotted the Fresno Piano Outlet just north of Ashlan Avenue. On a whim I pulled into the parking lot and moseyed on in. The bearded salesman showed me three pianos that were in my price range and then discreetly withdrew so that I could see and hear what they were like. One passed the audition with flying colors, and the next day I came back to buy it and arrange for it to be brought to my house.

The new instrument was a Ritmüller, and its power and expressive range were far superior to its predecessor's. The glistening keys, the pedals—all of it inspired me to integrate piano playing into my daily routine.

The felines, though, had a different sort of play in mind.

More than the instrument itself, the new upholstered piano bench caught their fancy. It was a glistening black, and it was over-the-top comfy. They could lounge there for hours at a time.

But none of them could be content with lounging alone.

Soon enough Oliver and Gulliver began playing regular rounds of "King of the Hill," using the piano bench as their central prop. It would start in a low-key way, with one of them getting on top of the bench and staring down on his rival. If cats can smirk, the king was definitely smirking at that point.

Then, of course, all bets were off as to how things would continue.

Let's say that Gulliver leaped onto the bench and appointed himself king this time. Oliver wouldn't say uncle, of course. He'd circle around the bench, looking for a way to get up to the coveted territory himself. When he found a likely place to make his ascent, he went for it—but Gulliver was on to him in an instant and pounded him back down. Game over? No way. Pride and desire wouldn't let Oliver withdraw and nurse his wounded ego. He tried again, and again, from other vantage points around the bench.

Feline brawls hardly began when the Ritmüller showed up here, of course. The cats have been going at it in other ways for years and years.

I've never felt the need to have a coffee table in the middle of the living room. All I've got there is a grand stretch of floor, with the recliner and the armchair and the sofa and some bookcases and the TV console hugging the walls. Now the piano has joined that lineup.

Danger is in the air and in Oliver's and Gulliver's eyes. They're gunning for each other, and neither one is about to stand down. They circle one another warily, their tails wafting to and fro in tense anticipation. Watching them from my armchair by the bay window, I'm reminded of scenes in spaghetti westerns like *The Good, The Bad, and the Ugly*. Before long this will turn nasty, and nothing can stop that from happening.

A few years ago, when my younger sister wound up living here for a while, she didn't have much trouble adjusting to the cats initially. Unlike our mother, she knows quite a bit about them. Over the years she's had a few as pets of her own, and she's absorbed far more book knowledge about them than I have.

On the other hand, Barbara's always only lived with one cat at a time. She's never had a pair or a group of them to look at and to look after.

When Oliver and Gulliver began their horseplay, she was caught off guard and appalled, then downright upset. Once she called out to me, "Make them stop it! Make them stop it!", not realizing that (a) this is all fairly typical and harmless feline behavior, and (b) I couldn't do much to forestall or break off their sparring in any case.

# MAT

In the mid-seventies I was an undergraduate at the University of the Pacific in Stockton. One afternoon, passing by Burns Tower and heading towards the library, I spotted a bearded someone on the lawn in a rigid lotus position, immersed in the business of meditation.

Flash forward to the early nineties. I heard about the California Vipassana Center up in North Fork, roughly a forty-minute drive from Fresno, and soon found myself applying for one of its introductory ten-day meditation retreats.

My first vipassana retreat was in the summer of 1995, and it cast a strong spell on me.

*Though the meditation itself was intriguing and intense, what also left its mark was the noble silence—the fact that, for ten full days, none of us at the retreat said anything to each other. We even avoided eye contact and gestures to each other. I'm not sure that I'll do another ten full days anytime soon—that wake-up gong at four o'clock each morning sounded a little too harsh sometimes—but I know that I'll go on shorter retreats from time to time. It seems to be an effective way, at least for me, to find some balance in what's often a rushed, chaotic flow of life experience.*

How did the retreat work? On the first evening, after all of the participants arrived and settled in, we were treated to a modest dinner and then a nuts-and-bolts orientation session in the main house. Staff members then took us to the spacious meditation hall and gave us bare-bones instructions about the way we were expected to meditate. Dovetailing with that was a brief practice period so that the coming days wouldn't seem completely foreign and bewildering to us.

We were housed in various cabins around the facility, about six per cabin, separated according to gender. One hardy soul volunteered to get up earlier than the rest of us—about a quarter to four—and march past all of the cabins every morning, banging an annoying but efficacious gong. According to the rules, we were all expected to find our way to the meditation hall by 4:30 AM for the day's first round of sitting.

Our guides referred to some other things during the orientation, but we only understood their full implications later on, when we came face-to-face with them. For example, following breakfast and an early lunch, no food was available in the afternoon or evening. Tea was on hand, but that was it. Something else that we heard about early on—"strong determination" meditations—only made real sense when they kicked in during the third or fourth day. During these periods we were all required to stay as rigid as statues for a full hour. Alone, I couldn't have gotten through them. It only worked because a few dozen other, earnest practitioners flanked me in the hall.

Meditation in this setting differed from the solo and small group sessions that I'd known up to that point. It turned out that intense meditation over several days brought an array of unexpected challenges. One afternoon, for whatever reason, the theme song from the *Hawaii Five-O* TV show jumped into my mind and then stayed there for hours. I couldn't shake it off, and there was a jarring disconnect between the bottomless silence enveloping me and those driving, annoying rhythms inside my head. It gave me a concrete understanding of what some Buddhist thinkers mean when they write about "monkey mind."

In the wake of that retreat I shelled out the bucks for my own meditation mat and zafu, a sturdy combo from the Shasta Abbey Buddhist Monastery.

Nowadays my practice has become far more casual than the strictures that the North Fork center mandated. I tend to start each day with a cup of coffee and at least twenty minutes on the zafu, give or take. I sit as placidly and mindfully as I can as I register this room, this space. Observed in virtual silence, it becomes a stranger again, a marvel, and a revelation.

Later on in the day some of the cats lay claim to the mat, and they make use of it for their own offbeat and antic forms of the contemplative art. Each has his own quirky, eccentric way of appropriating it.

When Oliver takes charge of the mat, he opts for a halfway-on, halfway-off position. His head and upper torso might be on top of it, but his hind legs and tail have spilled over onto the hardwood floor. Judging from the blissed-out expression on his face, though, he's reached a state of inner tranquility that I've rarely come across during my own zafu workouts.

Gulliver likes to adopt a more attentive and focussed pose. Thus ensconced, he stares out at the rest of the living room and takes it all in, studiously and intensely. Going by appearances, his is a level of concentration that I'll always aspire to but seldom equal.

Not that these guys ever seem to wrestle with metaphysical issues or existential vertigo. Their approach seems to reflect a contented acceptance of existence, a steadfast and placid embrace of each moment.

Removing cat hairs from the zafu and the mat has become a regular chore.

# Visits

Living with these guys is all well and good, but it can't always be neatly reconciled with one's romantic life.

One example should suffice.

It started out with a prosaic get-together—a movie and then coffee at a local Starbucks—and it moved in fits and starts to something more, something that caught both of us off guard.

She was also a teacher, a dedicated one like me, and so we settled on a fairly regular schedule to see each other—Thursday evenings and at least once every weekend.

From the very beginning that new plan, and the sundry activities that went along with it, didn't sit well with Tribble. Many times I wanted some privacy, meaning that Tribble found himself being unceremoniously removed from the house. More often than not he'd settled down on one of his favorite locations—the sofa, the bed—and he protested and resisted when I lifted him up and away. He didn't take this brazen and insulting treatment lying down, either. Sometimes, long after I'd removed him, we heard him climbing up the trellis in front of one of the windows. Soon enough he was peering at us through the glass and demanding that we let him back in. His ire only grew when he didn't get his way.

Falkor, bless his heart, was far more understanding and accommodating, but often just because of the furry coat that my visitor brought with her on nippy winter evenings. She'd drape it over the workout bench that I owned back then, and Falkor would make a pleasant nest for himself there. He curled up on top it dutifully, as if he wanted to protect it from cunning thieves. Sure enough, his sense of mission did the trick: the coat was always there, intact and secure, when she took her leave.

On other occasions, when I was gone for the evening or overnight,

I left extra food in the cat bowls and checked in with all of the animals before departing. Once again Tribble was visibly miffed. The orderly, predictable flow of time had been disrupted, and he liked order—the order that he'd grown used to—in the world around him. Beyond that, he probably felt sidelined, marginalized.

When I did show up in the house again, he gave me the silent treatment for a while, something that only gradually thawed and faded.

# Pizza

All cats will transform your living space in unusual and unexpected ways, but the prize in this category goes to Tribble, my Ur-cat, and something that happened way back in the late eighties when I was still a rookie cat person and newbie high school teacher.

It was a Thursday evening. The term had started a while back, and it was now settling down into a fairly predictable rhythm and speed.

It was time to celebrate one more week almost completed.

I called up a local pizza outfit, ordered a jumbo-sized Veggie Supreme, and waited for dinner to come to the door.

So far, so good.

But this was back when I was still naïve about cats, when I still made jumbo-sized errors of judgment about them. I'd gotten a cat tree for Tribble, a bulky thing that almost touched the ceiling. Given the oodles of time that he spent there, it clearly met with his approval. My mistake, though, was planting it right next to the dining room table.

After the pizza guy and I did our business, I brought the toasty cardboard box to the table, set it down, and flipped it open, never sensing the danger that lurked above me.

Tribble dove straight down into the pizza, landing there with a distinct thump. Extricating himself was no easy matter, given that I'd ordered extra cheese this time around. Whenever he pulled up one of his paws and made a bid for freedom, a ribbon of viscous cheese came up with him. The more he tried to free himself, the more the cheese spread over his front paws, face, and fur. The dilemma was beyond his ken, and it showed in his befuddled eyes and frantic meows. Only with my help could he get free, and cleaning him off thoroughly took the better part of an hour.

The cat tree found a new location in the apartment forthwith.

# Mindset

The presence of cats didn't just transform my living space, informing many places with fresh meaning and memories. It also altered my inner landscape—my set habits and routines.

During the eighties and nineties a bargain basement answering machine sat next to my landline. It took regular audiocassettes and let me record my own voice mail messages. As time went on, lots of them began to sport cat-oriented background music, including David Bowie's "Cat People" and Janet Jackson's "Black Cat."

Cat stuff insinuated itself into my consciousness in other ways as well.

Various segments from old TV shows began taking on new significance for me. One example: the "Catspaw" episode from the original *Star Trek* series. It kicked off with Kirk, Spock and McCoy coming across a trio of hags reciting lines from Shakespeare's *Macbeth*, and its twisty plot culminated when an alien sorceress morphed into a gigantic black cat—a Tribble clone—that stalked Kirk and Spock through dank castle hallways. Whenever the chance arises, I always check out that episode again.

My growing familiarity with cats also started to inform some of my work habits.

Many times, when I wrote up original exercises and stories for German classes, I drew on my own private tapestry of friends and close connections. Over time, though, cat-oriented material also became a regular feature— to the point that Tribble and his fellows got to be phantom presences in class. Now and then I shared anecdotes about Trib and his doings with my charges. After all, it was just another vehicle for using the language in everyday conversation.

Soon after I bought the house and moved in back in 1990, I started making jam and marmalade using fruit from the trees out back.

Soon—inevitably—the labels I came up with alluded to cats in general and my cohorts in particular. It made a peculiar kind of sense to me; after all, more often than not some or all of them were milling about close by when I was cooking up my concoctions, intrigued about what shenanigans I was up to this time. Hence the appearance of "A Catwork Orange," "Max and Moritz Marmalade," and "Gulliver's Peach Delight," among others.

Anne Bell, a friend whom I originally met during my time in Freiburg im Breisgau, began to get my concoctions each year. An accomplished artist, she's sometimes reciprocated by sending me some cat-themed work of hers. I can't help feeling that I've always gotten the better deal in that arrangement.

# THALHEIM

It was because of Tribble that, you might say, I saw "God."

Not only did I see "God," but I also got "God's" personal blessing, something that apparently undid the knots in my soul.

But I'm getting ahead of myself.

Let's scroll back to the middle of 2002, when my first Fulbright exchange year was set to take off. Lenny and Jerry had agreed to house Tribble during my year in Germany, and I needed to drive him up to their place on the coast.

When I brought Tribble up to their yurt close to Mendocino, glossy color photos of an Indian woman graced several walls, and a book about her occupied a prominent place on the living room table. Her name was Mother Meera, and my friends were both fascinated with her life story and her teachings. I hadn't heard about her before, but Lenny was more than happy to fill me in.

Mother Meera was said to be an avatar of the Divine Mother and hence a divine being. She'd come into the world to open people to the Light of Paramatman, the Supreme Being. The ceremony of darshan played a key part in this process. During this occasion seekers bowed before her, and she touched the back of their necks. Her potent touch helped to foster the activity of the Light.

Words like avatar were a little too abstruse for me, so I just found myself thinking of her as a god, or simply "God."

Her base of operations was Thalheim, a modest farming community close to Frankfurt am Main in Germany—and not all that far away from Düsseldorf, where I'd be living and working.

I listened politely, and later on I flipped through a Mother Meera paperback they had, but what I picked up didn't resonate all that much with me. Many of Mother Meera's observations resembled sentiments that I'd seen elsewhere, and her thoughts always seemed to be epithets, nothing that probed issues deeply and thoroughly. It didn't help either, that her name reminded me of an oddball episode of a sixties spy series called *The Girl from U.N.C.L.E.*, the one in which April Dancer and Napoleon Solo faced off against their latest nemesis—Mother Muffin, played in drag by Boris Karloff. As I tried to concentrate on Meera's perspective and message, images of that episode flitted across my mind.

Lenny and Jerry, naturally, encouraged me to visit her center in Thalheim during my stint overseas, something I wasn't totally averse to. After all, the whole point of traveling overseas like this was to seek out and explore the new, the novel.

When I landed in Düsseldorf in July 2002, my Fulbright exchange partner picked me up from the airport, and a few days later we went to an orientation session in Bad Godesberg. Shortly after that she was winging her way to her California adventure, and her apartment became mine for the duration. One morning I dropped by my new workplace, the *Heinrich Heine Gesamtschule,* and introduced myself to Gerd Heesen, the principal. The official start of the new term was still a few weeks off, though, and there wasn't much for me to do at the school until then.

Among other things, that interlude gave me time to give "God" a call.

There was a phone booth close to my apartment building, and back then—before the advent of ubiquitous cell phones—that was the simplest way for me to dial the Thalheim number that Lenny and Jerry had given me. The German ring tone sounded a few times, and then someone picked up—not "God" herself, but apparently one of her acolytes, and one who spoke fluent German to boot. I explained my interest in visiting Mother Meera, omitting some key parts of the backstory—for example, that an overweight black cat figured prominently in all of this. I learned that Mother Meera regularly held a darshan on Sunday evenings throughout the year. I jotted down the information he gave me, added it to a folder back in the apartment, and let my friends in California know that I'd made contact.

And then weeks and months passed by, jam-packed with other things.

The demands of the school schedule thundered down on me, and thoughts of escaping to Thalheim some Sunday evening were relegated to the back burner, then taken away from the stove completely for a while. As the months passed, I grew increasingly reluctant to actually go through with the trip. Though some of what I'd heard in Mendocino piqued my interest, nothing in the Meera material that I'd looked at spoke to me in a particularly inspiring way. Granted, some of it was intriguing—and an opportunity like this wasn't likely to come my way later on—but I didn't feel compelled to pursue the matter. And so, as my hesitation grew and my reluctance festered, I put off plans to get over there.

Lenny still hoped that I'd be able to work in a visit. In early March she wrote that *Mother Meera was going to come to San Francisco in June, but now she's not. Jerry and I were really looking forward to it…Please, if you can, go as my proxy (or even for yourself) and let me know what the direct experience is like.*

Soon after that I wrote to let them know that Thalheim was no longer in the cards.

*As it turns out, I probably won't be seeing Mother Meera. Hopefully you can understand why. If you were coming to Germany—or, for example, if Reiner and Ulla, two colleagues of mine, wanted to go—it'd be a different story. With so little time remaining, I'd rather spend time with the people I've met in Düsseldorf or get on the road to other cities.*

Then things did an abrupt about-face. In early May Reiner Böhnlein, the school psychologist, let me know that he definitely wanted to go to Thalheim with me. His enthusiasm was infectious, and we soon figured out a day that would work for both of us.

I phoned the Thalheim number once again and made some arrangements.

*Dear Lenny and Jerry,*

*Thought you should know that I'll be seeing Mother Meera, if all goes as planned, on June 19ᵗʰ. Reiner Böhnlein, a friend from the school, will be coming along. Am going as a proxy for both of you, but also as a proxy for some people around here who (because of what I told them about what you told me), are curious about MM as well.*

In late May they sent me two books with more background intel.

*Thanks for the books, which were a nice surprise in my mailbox this afternoon. Have let my neighbors, Elmar and Uschi, borrow Answers while I check out (at least parts of) Hidden Journey.*

As a rule, most of the people you work with at a school don't become dear friends. They're colleagues, and they stay that way. They can be great for small talk and scuttlebutt in the copy room, but they rarely become closer than that over the long haul. That's what makes the exceptions so special and so memorable. Reiner Böhnlein did yeoman's service for me during my year in Düsseldorf, taking the time to help me out with an especially unruly sixth-grade group, the notorious 6.5 class. He was a thoughtful man, a keen observer, and traveling to the darshan with him would make that occasion a lot more meaningful.

On June 19th Reiner swung by my apartment building in the early afternoon. Our plan was to rocket down to Thalheim and rendezvous with the other darshan participants close to the train station there, as we'd been instructed to do. The drive was smooth and picturesque, but it took longer than we'd expected—so much so that, when we finally pulled up in front of the meeting place, it was deserted. We scouted around the area and buttonholed a few locals; they let us know that Mother Meera's helpers had met with the others about fifteen minutes ago and taken them to the building where the darshan was actually being held. They pointed us in the right direction, and off we went.

Being tardy was embarrassing enough, but things got worse. When we found the address and stepped up to the front door, it was closed and locked. We had no choice but to use the doorbell, one that buzzed raucously.

An attendant let us in.

Inside all of the other participants—thirty, forty—were already seated in lotus positions in front of Mother Meera, who presided over them from her place of honor in front of a row of shimmering windows. All of them watched us in pristine silence, Mother included, as we sheepishly found a place to sit down and get settled. Her eyes were serene and compassionate. Her demeanor radiated a profound energy, one unmoved and unperturbed by negligible matters like our gauche entrance.

Unlike other spiritual retreats I've attended, this one lacked anything like a sermon, discussion, or Q and A session. A steady, intense quiet governed the evening's proceedings, and the program was unvarnished and straightforward. Our task was to sit in meditation, using whatever meditative technique we felt comfortable with. Then, when one of us felt an inner pull, or call, that person would approach Mother Meera and bow deeply in front of her. She would then put her hands on the nape of that person's neck and undo the knots in that person's soul. The session unfolded in a surprisingly orderly way, given that most of us were clearly here for the first time, and given that things got off to an awkward start after Reiner and I had made our ill-timed entrance.

After the ceremony came to a close, the evening wrapped up in slow motion. Knots of people gathered here and there in the meeting hall or in the hallway outside, and some picked up Meera merchandise from a large table featuring the stuff.

Reiner and I found our way outside and decided we needed to share our impressions and debrief before heading back to Düsseldorf. We found a wooded area close by, one laced with park benches and lengthening shadows. Our conclusions? Most of all the sense of searching impressed us. Those who had come to this ceremony, or communal blessing, had that special look in their eyes, a yearning to find something more profound, something that reached beyond the surface of their lives. The diversity of that crowd—in terms of age, social class, ethnicity—also stirred us. Was it worth it to get over to Thalheim? Yes, it was, especially given that Reiner, a good friend, had been able to come along and share the experience.

The drive back to Düsseldorf was an uneventful blur, marked by the orderly, well-lighted efficiency of the *Autobahn*.

It was close to midnight when Reiner dropped me off at my apartment building. After I stepped out of the elevator and into my place, I called up Mendocino. The time difference wasn't a problem; it was afternoon in Lenny and Jerry's slice of the world.

When they wanted to know how I felt about seeing Mother Meera up close and witnessing one of her darshans. I told them what Reiner and I had talked about in our post-meeting session. We'd both been moved by the atmosphere of the place, by the sorts of people—seekers—who were genuinely drawn to this woman's presence and the promise of her spiritual message. Some moments bothered and annoyed me, of course—like that Meera promo table and its extensive array of literature and occasionally frivolous knickknacks.

The visit had been worthwhile, I decided again when thinking about it all later. On the other hand, it led me to consider other sources of spiritual inspiration that I'd encountered recently—like the fifth-grade English class I was teaching that year. Again and again, that group's spontaneity and vitality proved to be a delight and an inspiration. Once, right before spring break, I was teaching them in their ground-floor room, whose windows looked out onto a lush sun-drenched meadow. When a rabbit suddenly appeared out there, the whole class scrambled over to the windows to check it out. "Look, Mr. Roesch!" one of them called out in nearly perfect English. "It is the Easter bunny." That moment in time beat the darshan hands down.

Mother Meera had a powerful aura and gravitas. Her gaze was deep and probing. Much the same holds, though, for the feline eyes that shine on me around here. Truly, I get a taste of Thalheim day after day—in their eyes, in their apparent feats of concentration on the meditation mat, in the beauty of their movements and their endearing ways.

And also in their touch.

Oliver's hand-licking surely qualifies as a blessing of the first order. Tribble's famous face pushes certainly qualified as well. So does the way that Moritz plays "Apricot Tree" and "Lectern" with me many times each week, and so did Falkor when he settled down around my neck while I was reading in the recliner.

Even the way that Ramses once thoughtfully brought me a mouse he'd disposed of, laying it down on the mat by the back door—that qualifies as well.

All in all, as it turns out, Mother Meera and those like her have some significant competition.

# Wound

An overcast weekday, and a hectic one. I've got a row of online classes lined up, which means that the felines need to get their grub a half an hour earlier than usual. It's nothing that they'll yowl about, naturally, and when I bring their wet food they've already staked out their positions, the way chess pieces stand in their regular spots at the onset of a game.

Except that there's something odd about Maxwell today, something I can't pinpoint right away. His black and white fur seems more unkempt than usual. He's gotten over to his bowl, all right, but he's moving sluggishly. As I spoon some pungent wet stuff into his bowl, I notice the open wound over his right eye. It's the sort of gash that a cat fight probably caused, and it needs attention.

I go inside to grab a washcloth and get some soapy water. When I return, Maxwell's still lingering over his bowl at the tail end of his meal. I grab him under his chin and draw him away from his food—something he's less than enthusiastic about—and clean the area as best I can. Treating his wound, though, calms him down. He seems to realize that this is something salutary for him, and he stops fidgeting and accepts my ministrations.

Back in the house I find the number of my go-to vet clinic. Sure enough, they've got an opening for tomorrow at 9:40 AM. COVID protocols are now in place, meaning that I'll need to drive Maxwell to their back parking lot and then phone their receptionist on my cell. I'll have to wait in the Golf until one of the vet techs comes out and lets me bring him in.

Maxwell's strictly an outdoor cat, so in his case a vet visit is never a simple–as–pie operation. I lay the groundwork in the evening, clearing some random things from the spare bedroom and hauling in a water bowl, filled to the brim, as well as some dry cat food in a silvery bowl. Both sit on a fuzzy blue bath towel underneath the window. I also lug in a litter box, properly filled, and set that down kitty-corner from the other items.

On the following morning I bring out food for the outdoor felines, and of course Maxwell's there on his customary perch atop the blue recycling bin, ready to partake. He suspects nothing. Not realizing that today will be different from other days, he sinks his head into his bowl and feeds himself with intense abandon. After I've taken care of the indoor pair, especially Gulliver, I slip back outside, approach Maxwell stealthily, and—quickly, because speed and surprise are key—lift him up and then towards the back door. He's been blindsided, his paws do a frantic dance on the air, but it's far too late for effective resistance.

I bring him into the spare bedroom with its new cat-friendly accouterments and then linger for a time, just holding him as he peers around this strange room with wide and wondering eyes. Soon he looks docile and accepting, but that's either a bluff or a phase. After I shut the door firmly behind me, he starts to scramble up the Venetian blinds like a maniac.

I go inside again. He's sprawled against the window, his claws gripping the check rail. I take him away from his frenzied pose, gently yet firmly, and bring him back to the spare bed. Then I raise the blinds all the way to the top before spending even more time in there to calm him down and soothe his nerves.

In the course of the next few hours, before we have to leave for his appointment, I still hear him scrambling around in there now and then.

Show time at the pet hospital is fast approaching. I park in the back and phone the office, and soon a vet tech taps on my car window. Following her inside with Maxwell in the carrier is a proverbial piece of cake, as is the initial phase in the examination room.

During this time I give her the *CliffsNotes* version of the Maxwell saga. He's a stray who's chosen to spend the lion's share of his time on my property, especially in the forlorn nooks and crannies of my garage. He doesn't seem to be getting fed by anyone else; certainly no one else has been getting vet care for his facial injury. I confess that I don't even know 100 percent if we're dealing with a male or a female here, and whether or not this one has actual owners is also the stuff of speculation. She brings in a cell phone–sized scanner to check for an implant, comes up blank, then moves it over him a second and third time to double and triple check. No implant. A peek at his groin and she can report that we're dealing with a male here—something that I'd assumed given his interactions with the others in the backyard.

Maxwell behaves himself reasonably well during the vet's pre-examination routine, even when he's forced to hold still on the scale and when a thermometer is slipped into his posterior for a seemingly interminable time. Fortunately those readings turn out to be normal.

For a while—say, fifteen minutes this time around—Maxwell and I are then left to our own devices in the examination room, awaiting the vet's arrival. A window behind us has been tipped open, and it lets in a subtle breeze as well as the swoosh and occasional roar of Shields Avenue traffic. Checking out the financial section in *The Economist* seems inappropriate right now. It's vital to hold Maxwell close and keep his anxiety in check. As I cradle him on my lap, his anxious eyes scan the room—its off-white ceiling panels, the splash of pet-related advertising on the bulletin board next to the spartan office clock.

The vet who now appears is someone I know well, a soft-spoken and bespectacled Asian. He's impressed with the care I took to keep Maxwell's wound clean, and he prescribes an oral antibiotic and an iodine solution that I should use twice each day over the coming ten days.

So ended a smooth fairy tale vet visit.

But not all of them work out that way.

# GETAWAY

When they're out and about in public, parents want their children to act well. They cringe, at least on the inside, when their kids exhibit less than exemplary behaviors.

The same holds true for us cat owners. I always want my guys to be on good behavior when we go to the vet. When those hopes founder, my heart sinks and my spirits plummet.

Now and then, of course, the misdeed is a mere peccadillo. It's quickly over and done with, something that the vet and his staff and I can have a good laugh about.

Like the time that I took Ramses in for his annual physical exam and shots.

When I packed him into the carrier that day, Ramses was edgy and agitated. I noticed the telltale signs, but figured that nothing would go awry. And, indeed, the first phase of the exam proceeded without incident. Then he needed to be weighed. Just as the vet tech was lifting him onto the scale, the door swung open, the vet came in—and Ramses spotted a chance to make his getaway.

He squirmed away from the vet tech, scrammed toward the door, and skedaddled down the hallway. A madcap pursuit ensued, and he almost made it to the other end of the clinic before the staff cornered him and got him under control.

But that misconduct was low key, with a low reading on the I'm–ashamed–of–my–pet's–behavior dial.

# PAW

Sometimes vet appointments don't wind up as disasters, if only because of unexpected peripeties.

Moritz presents a case in point.

He was in the flower bed by the garage, lying on his side with a dull, glazed stare that belied his usual perkiness. I bent down and rubbed his back, then his belly. He roused himself, arching his back as all cats tend to do. When he started coming out into the sunlight, it looked like he was limping. I scooped him up and felt along his back legs. One of them, the left one, seemed to have shrunk somehow. The claws weren't visible there, unlike the appearance of the right paw. The left one was flatter, the fur duller. When I ran my hands lightly over both paws, though, he didn't mind; he didn't wince and he didn't pull back.

Time, of course, to bring him to the animal hospital. I left a message on their voice mail, asking for the earliest possible slot on Monday. Then I treated Moritz to some wet food, something he wolfed down sedulously. Whatever had happened to him, it hadn't downsized his appetite.

Is the bleak news at fault? On Monday I'm hopelessly awake at 4:30 AM. I busy myself with sundry chores and read even more headlines—more about mass shootings in Wisconsin and Indiana—before prepping for kitty food time. Today there are some additions to the regular, well-worn routine. My hope is to get Moritz to the vet before noon. I'm counting on the pet hospital to find time for him, the sooner the better. That in turn means that I can't just blithely bring out his food and fill his dish and let him be. I'll need to get him inside and keep him there—something he won't stomach without fiery resistance.

Once again I prepare the spare bedroom, bringing in a water bowl and a food bowl, plus a freshly replenished litter box. I take care to raise all of the Venetian blinds as far as they can go, knowing from abundant experience that if I omit this step, the imprisoned cat (or guest, as I like to think of him) will be clambering up them once I spring the trap. In no time at all the blinds would be a tortured chaos of slats.

Once I've prepared the holding cell (or guest room, as I like to think of it) I feed the whole lot—except for Maxwell, who hasn't deigned to show his fuzzy, quizzical face quite yet. Then I cradle Moritz in my arms and bring him inside and into his temporary quarters. Sure enough, he's howling and yowling in nanoseconds, and even the bountiful extra helping of dry food in that spiffy food bowl does little to assuage his bile and indignation.

Some tasks occupy my attention for half an hour or so—emails that need responses, online classes that urgently need to be prepared for—and then I figure that it's time to pay Moritz a visit. I need to let him know that, contrary to appearances, he's loved and he's cherished. Getting inside the guest room requires finesse, because just swinging the door open will prompt a bold escape followed by a raucous chase through all nooks, corners and crannies of the house. I just push the door open a tad, enough to look through the pencil-thin slit and make sure that he's not hanging out right at the threshold. Before opening up any further, I make some ridiculous-sounding "Sh! Sh!" noises which, improbably, send most of my cats, Moritz included, scurrying away in dread.

He not only retreats, but slips way back beneath the bed, so I've got to coax him out and then hold him again in my arms. His front paws hang over my forearm in a position that lets me (a) mollify him, and (b) examine his hind legs again. Funny thing, though—now they pretty much match each other, and the alarm signals that went off yesterday aren't speaking up anymore.

A test is called for. I set him down on the hardwood floor, go over to the door, and ask him to come over toward me. Nothing doing, though, as I should have anticipated. This whole procedure—bringing him into this austere room and locking him inside, then leaving him there unattended for a while, then bursting inside with repugnant "Sh!" noises—has left him bewildered. All he can do is look at me blankly, probably at a loss to know what this guy will do next. At last, though, after some prompting— also modelling, because I start to pace back and forth to demonstrate what I want from him—he follows suit, and I notice to my surprise that, remarkably, he isn't limping at all anymore.

And so I've got no real choice but to pull the door open. For a moment I get the feeling that I might have acted too soon, and that maybe he'll take the opportunity to rush pell-mell through all of the other rooms. He's focussed on going outside, though. Once he gets his bearings, he makes a bee line for the kitchen, where I can let him out into freedom's realm. Not surprisingly he elects not to linger by the back steps—who knows what this lunatic owner will want from him next?—but rather to get some distance from the back door and from me. Then, as I saunter out after him, he bounds away even further, reasoning that prudence dictates a fair amount of distance in these circumstances.

The pet hospital gets another voice mail from me, this time letting them know that Moritz won't need an appointment after all. The cryptic ways of his constitution have made themselves felt once again.

# CHECKUP

Up to that time Moritz had an impeccable good citizenship record from the vet, but that wasn't destined to last.

The close of July was fast approaching, time for the guy's annual checkup and shots. I called them again and, lo and behold, they had an opening later that day at 3:30 PM, meaning that I had to use no small measure of craft and stealth to get him there on time.

Usually the cats get some morsels smack in the middle of the afternoon, but today I delayed their munchies until a little after three. It wasn't easy, given the way they were eyeballing me through the kitchen window. Eventually I served all of them, even the neurotically peripatetic Maxwell. This time I had to hunt that one down, bowl of consumables in hand, and then persuade him, with strategic strokes of affection, to start consuming.

Following that it was time to prep for Operation Checkup. Wallet with credit card? Check. Latest edition of *The Economist* to flip through in case there was some waiting time? Check. Cat carrier at the ready? Not quite. I turned the carrier on its end so that its open mouth was now facing upward, waiting to receive an inmate.

I stepped outside again, found Moritz contemplating his already empty bowl with wide-open, disbelieving eyes, and then scooped him up and carried him up the back steps. Once inside I tried, in one swift motion, to drop him down into the carrier.

True to his rambunctious nature, though, Moritz would not go gently into that dark space. He struggled mightily against my designs, grabbing at the grid of the door, meowing his complaints with a crescendo of indignation—but within half a minute I forced him down into the bowels of the carrier, shut the door, and secured it. For good measure I tested the door a few times to make sure that it was locked tight. One of my recurring anxieties is that I don't secure it well enough and that, when I get to the vet's office, the cat inside breaks out, vamooses, and can never be found again.

This time the place was unusually quiet. Typically some other pet owners are milling around at the front counter. Today it was just me—and a rankled Moritz kvetching from inside his confines, of course. One of the vet techs got my name, double-checked the appointment list, and directed me to Room Two, where I coaxed the reluctant patient onto the examination table. His eyes seemed twice as large as usual as they swept around the room. They seemed especially intrigued by the corners around the ceiling, as if gremlins up there were glaring down at him and wishing him ill. His agitation didn't let up, and I wound up bringing him over to a plastic chair by the windows, where I tried, not quite successfully, to keep him in my arms and settle him down. In many cases, when you treat a cat this way, he'll lie down in one position, then shift to a comfier one, then gradually pipe down. Today, though, Moritz's nerves wouldn't let him chill—a harbinger that didn't bode well.

When the tech came in, I held Moritz steady as she took his temperature rectally—another indecency that no doubt confirmed his deepest suspicions and misgivings. Next she got his weight—something that, given his anxious fidgeting, required multiple attempts. Before she left, she let us know that the vet would be in shortly—which turned out to be inaccurate, maybe because the place was understaffed in these coronavirus times. Once more I sat him down on my lap and tried assuage his concerns. It hit me that I usually never hold him this long and this close. Moritz is a fiercely independent soul, a spirit of the suburban outdoors, and though he invites me to pet him now and then, he only courts those PDAs on his own terms, and typically just for fairly brief intervals.

In times like these I recognize the scope and depth of these animals' role in my life. It's something that I take for granted again and again; the familiar routines of the everyday have a way of obscuring these connections. When the vet tech mentioned, off the cuff, that Moritz was now eight years old, I winced. Some animals, Moritz included, don't betray their age that readily. He still such a nimble guy, whether he's scampering after a cat intruder or just merrily racing around the yard, beckoning me to give chase in a lively session of cat tag. Eight years already?

When the vet joined us, the actual checkup unfolded by the numbers—at least for a while. Moritz got a clean bill of health. His ears, teeth, tummy, and other essentials were all in working order. His coat of fur looked decent, too. And so the appointment could have ended on a positive and celebratory note. But then his mood darkened.

Just before the examination wrapped up, he complained loudly about the way he was being held and handled. Then, without warning, he sprang off the table, shot underneath a chest of drawers by the window, and crawled as far to the rear as he could manage—too far back for any of us to get a hold of him and bring him back out, that was for sure.

One of the vet techs disappeared for moment. When she got back, she was brandishing a net with an extra-long handle. She kneeled down next to his hideaway, fiddled with the net for a time—the culprit wasn't making her task an easy one—and finally brought him out, still struggling against his confinement. Somehow the three of us were able to get him into the carrier again. When one of the staff came in with my bill minutes later, I offered to include a tip for their troubles, but she declined, claiming it was against their policy.

The trip back home took well under ten minutes, yet Moritz was beside himself with fury the whole time. Only after I swung open the hatchback, brought the carrier out into the yard, and opened up the grated door, did his displeasure subside. Bullets don't leave the business end of pistols faster than some cats exit their carriers, and before I knew it Moritz was comfortably installed with his peers again. He shook himself a few times—the only indication that he'd just survived an onerous ordeal.

# Mood Swings

Misery might love company, but so does notoriety. Around the same time Gulliver needed to get his annual checkup, and he wound up aping Moritz's M.O.

Again, I should have seen it coming. The summer of Gulliver's discontent should have been obvious. A few weeks earlier, for example, both tabbies were lounging on the bedspread while I was wrapping up some tasks at my desk. It was one of those moments when I felt (a) proud to have such delightful cat company, and (b) grateful for having bought a queen-sized mattress several years ago, because this way there'd be a sliver of space for me over there in a while.

Out of the blue, though, Gulliver began growling. First it was a mezzo piano grumbling aimed at Oliver, one that his pugnacious glare underscored. Then his grumbling started an ominous crescendo, and his eyes now spoke daggers and rapiers to his brother tabby. Soon enough Oliver got the message and decided to look for a safe haven elsewhere. He got up from his cozy pose, shook himself a bit to get fully awake—to me it looked as if he was shaking his head about Gulliver's unreasonableness—and then stood for a time on the edge of the bed, looking down at the floor as if he were wondering if, really and truly, all of this was truly warranted. Gulliver's admonitory noises weren't letting up at all, though, so he leapt down to the floor and left his bro to his own devices.

Gulliver began to show similar spells of irascibility when I was teaching my Zoom and Skype lessons. Now and then, as was my wont, I gesticulated to my online students to emphasize some points. All of that worked well—unless, of course, Gulliver had gotten on top of the Canon printer to my right. Sometimes my motions grew more animated and pronounced, and—not that I realized it—they were encroaching on his private space.

He took umbrage at my audacity, and he wasn't willing to let it slide. When he struck, it was always without warning, his paw lashing out at me several times in a quick staccato attack. More than once I had to let my virtual audience know what was going on: that an off-screen cat had just clobbered me.

Before too long, needless to say, he became cat non grata in the study during my remote teaching sessions. But that cantankerousness was still festering within him, liable to come out of the shadows at a moment's—or a hand's—notice.

Or when it was his turn to go to the vet.

First, everything was as smooth as a spring breeze. Gulliver bellyached during the drive over to the clinic, as always, but once we got inside, he grew reticent and compliant.

The start of the examination was auspicious. Gulliver let himself get extracted from the carrier. He stood attentively on the examination table, and given how alert and observant he was, he seemed eager to go along with all of our wishes.

Then something struck him the wrong way, though what provoked his moodiness wasn't clear. While the vet was checking out his teeth and listening to his heartbeat, he suddenly decided that he'd had enough of this nonsense. He started to act out, first with his staple low growls and then louder and louder still. Soon enough he was hissing at the staff like a demon and swiping at them with no-nonsense paw strikes.

The staff called in some backup, and four extra hands soon restrained Gulliver for the rest of his exam. The spring breeze had dissipated, and a troubled, overcast ambience took hold.

Bottom line: both Moritz and Gulliver have now earned a special mark in their files. When I get an appointment for either of them nowadays, I also have to pick up a tranquilizer to give them orally an hour before their scheduled time. When I come in these days with either of them in tow, I always get the key questions: Did I administer the tranquilizer, and if so, did I do it in a timely way?

When it comes to the animal hospital, these two are now definitely in the doghouse.

To date this arrangement has spared us further misconduct and embarrassment, but who can tell what the future holds?

# ABSENCES

It's something that you dread, and it's something that happens ineluctably.

Morning arises, full of latent possibilities. Before you know it, it's time to give the assorted felines their grub—but one of them is missing.

Now and then the mystery of a cat's disappearance only stays mysterious for a sliver of time. Once, in the nineties, Tribble was nowhere to be found—but then, after a few hours, he was somewhere to be heard, namely in my neighbor's place. While I was watering the rosebushes out back that afternoon, I noticed his distinct yammering—not so much a call of the wild as a call of wild dismay—and it was definitely coming from Augie's garage.

When I rang Augie's doorbell and let him know where Tribble was trapped, he seemed dubious at first. Sure enough, though, when he pulled his garage door open, a familiar bundle of fur was cowering underneath his workbench, tense and agitated. As soon as Tribble detected a way to get out of that space without passing too close to us, he took his chances and fled into the driveway, then back over the chain-link fence and into my yard.

Another time, a similar outcome. Tribble wasn't to be found—and someone with his proportions is tough to miss. Soon enough, though, I heard his plaintive cries once again, this time emanating from underneath the house.

Earlier on I'd been cleaning around the entry to the crawl space. The lid must have been ajar and the entry unattended for a moment, but that was enough time for Trib to do some amateur spelunking. Curiosity didn't kill the cat this time, but it definitely did a number on his usually stately appearance. When Tribble scrambled out of the crawl space, he wore a thick coat of pungent dirt and sticky cobwebs, not to mention a sour and irascible attitude. No lasting harm was done, though, and soon all was back to normal in the Roesch Estate.

On April 17, 2021, it happened again. When the missing party is located without too much trouble, no problem. If the situation drags on, though, it begins to gnaw at me.

When I went out to feed the felines, one of them wasn't around. This time it was Moritz, the one who typically was always present and accounted for at every mealtime. Like a model grade school student, Moritz would always show up, bright and perky, and he'd be civilly insistent about his need to get his food pronto.

But this Saturday morning didn't fit that pattern. Moritz's black form was nowhere to be seen or heard. Also—and this has always irked me about my crew—none of the others seemed to notice or mind. Maxwell, licking heartily at his food, was especially cool with being solo on top of the recycling container. His longtime breakfast pal was AWOL, but hey—that didn't cramp his eating style at all.

For me, though, it was another story. Moritz's absence was present throughout the morning, even as I scanned online news articles and editorials, even as I taught some online English and chess sessions. More than a few times, between classes, I found myself in the garden again, touring Moritz's most beloved hiding and snoozing places—especially underneath the towering cypresses that stand guard by the front of the garage. Nothing doing. He wasn't in any of those hangouts, but I kept looking now and again because I didn't want to believe what might well be the case—that Moritz would now be gone for good.

In the early afternoon Oliver unexpectedly rose from his cherished spot in the spare bedroom and sauntered over to the back door. His insistent eye contact with me signaled that he wanted out. As I abided by his wishes, I leaned down and told him to "Find Moritz."

A deepening sting of loss only got stronger as the hours slouched by. In a way it was surprising that my reaction should be so pronounced. After all, I'd been on this same merry-go-round of emotions many times before. But it was Moritz this time, Max's loyal and affectionate brother and comrade in arms, the one who treasured Otto Linberger's aged classroom podium almost as much as I did.

Sometimes the waiting stretches from one day into the next and then onward. The absence becomes something solid, as palpable as a gravestone.

But not this time around.

It was going on three in the afternoon. Moritz still wasn't readily visible anywhere, but that didn't deter me from looking behind rosebushes and other sundry garden plants—and those were his eyes gleaming in the flower bed, right behind the Linberger lectern.

When he noticed me noticing him, he stretched his front paws way out in front of him and extended his back legs as far back as they would go— an invitation that he wanted my attention, and lots of it, and right away. No explanation about his absence would ever be forthcoming, of course.

# TREE

Several years ago the internet featured a video that someone in Germany had made about his cat's perambulations through the neighborhood. A tinkering sort, he fastened a compact camera to a specially designed collar and secured it around his pet's neck. He let the cat out early one morning, and his cat stayed away, as usual, for most of the day.

Later, when he looked at the video from the camera, he could see just how far his pet had ventured—well over two kilometers—and just how many others, animals as well as humans, it had interacted with. It made me wonder about my own felines and their daily excursions. Only occasionally do I get a glimpse of what they've been up to—like the time a few years ago when Oliver disappeared for a few days.

This was back in 2018. Barbara, my younger sister, was staying in the spare bedroom at the time, and early on she made friends with all of the cats, especially Oliver. And why not? When I needed to find a replacement for Lorenzo, she'd come along to the adoption center with me and helped me pick Oliver and name him. Their bond soon became close and solid.

I took note of Oliver's absence, of course, and it concerned me, but Barbara really noticed it and took it to heart. One day slipped by, then another. Once, when I went into the kitchen to wash some dishes, I found her there, her eyes wet with tears and anguish. Oliver was still gone, and she was a wreck because of it.

I did a reconnaissance of the neighborhood, knocking on doors and even putting up some flyers with Oliver's mug and my phone number on telephone poles. No helpful tips came our way.

All seemed lost.

It was getting toward spring, high time to start pruning the fruit trees. I carried a ladder out of the garage, set it up next to the apricot tree, and got to the task at hand. Soon, though, after I started trimming the upper branches, a familiar sound came my way.

It was like the time when I heard Tribble crying out from Augie's garage, and then a few months later when he called out from the depths of the crawl space. Now, though, it wasn't Tribble anymore. It was definitely Oliver. I'd recognize that jumbo-sized voice anywhere. He was in one of the lots to the north of mine, across the alley and up in a mammoth tree.

I called over to him. He stopped for a moment—maybe because he recognized me?—and then he started hollering again. An ominous sign: a number of dogs were also over there, barking viciously like a crazed mob.

It was time to put my pruning duties on hold. I went over to the next street, knocked on a few doors—now that I was on the parallel street it wasn't quite clear to me which lot held the tree in question—and struck out on my first attempt. It looked like no one was home anywhere—except for that pack of noisy dogs, of course, and except for one frenzied cat.

Later that morning I made a second try at one of the houses, and this time a middle-aged Hispanic man opened up. I told him what was up, and he led me along some carpeted corridors and then past a screen door into the yard. Two dogs—amiable and benign, from the looks of them—greeted us as we stepped outside, but the four others circling the tree trunk were a rough crowd, barking up a storm and keeping Oliver, who was high above them, in his place and in his state of abject panic.

I asked my neighbor if he had a ladder, and he not only obliged me by bringing one from his garage, but also insisted on clambering up it himself. Oliver, uncertain about this guy's intentions, tried to keep some distance between himself and this new possible menace, meaning that my neighbor had to leave the ladder and work his way along one of the branches. Some leaves rustled, some hard–to–interpret noises sounded, but soon enough the rescue operation was a success. Holding Oliver firmly against his chest with one hand, he got himself down the ladder with the other, where he handed Oliver over to me.

Mission accomplished—except, of course, that getting this tabby back to safe and familiar ground still lay before me. I whisked him along the oak-lined sidewalk, then ducked down the alley back to my street, but all the while Oliver was struggling mightily against my hold. It was all that I could do to keep him wrapped in my arms, trapped and secure.

Being held at bay for hours by baying dogs had scared him to no end, and that fear made him want to bolt at all costs. It wasn't easy, but I made it back to my own front door with my load still with me. But the doorbell didn't bring Barbara. Whatever she was doing, it was poor timing writ large. I hurried around to the back door and somehow kept Oliver under control while fishing my house keys out of my pocket. Once the door was unlocked, I tossed Oliver inside, then got in myself and secured the door behind me. The familiar walls and furnishings caught him by surprise, then settled him down.

Barbara, as it turned out, wasn't in the house, but once she got back from her walk the "mother and child reunion" was complete. That evening I knocked on her door, and when she told me I could come in I found her crossed-legged on her bed and in much improved spirits. A winsome Oliver lay beside her, looking at me with a matter-of-fact equanimity.

Oliver wasn't wearing a camera on his collar that day, but for once I'd gotten a sense of the adventures and hijinks that my cats get themselves caught up in once in a while. Happily, most of their exploits end without much drama and trauma. One wonders what made Oliver explore that particular yard in the first place, given that it was chock-full of aggressive dogs, but it became clear to me then that he's far more than a mouth with an endless appetite. He's also an intrepid and fearless soul, and a mishap like this one doesn't deter him from regular, far-flung excursions.

# Test

Sometimes a cat's disappearing act doesn't seem to arise from some accident or misfortune, but because of cunning intent. Maybe I'm off the mark here, but now and then it looks as if these cats have their own agenda when they vanish the way they do.

It's happened at least a dozen times, and it's happened with Tribble, Falkor...pretty much all of the ones who have had access to the house. All of a sudden one of them seems to have melted into space. He was definitely inside, so I know that he must still be there somewhere, but where? And so the hunt is afoot.

My home has modest dimensions, so in theory this puzzle shouldn't be much of a head-scratcher. All of the felines have an uncanny knack for finding hiding places among the stuff in my closets, so I rummage through all of them with zealous care. I get down on all fours and peer underneath the beds in both bedrooms—another favorite feline hideaway.

Yet another perennial favorite: the space beneath the living room recliner. Sometimes, right off the bat, I've hit the jackpot—a live, reclusive cat—but on other occasions all I've found was a nest of dust bunnies down there. After I got the new piano, I kept it a tad removed from the wall, and so—conceivably, possibly—one of them might be hanging out behind the Ritmüller.

Another trick that some of them land on now and then: the bookcases that I've set close to, but not flush with, two corners of the living room. There they can also wait, listen, and see if, finally, at long last, I can figure out where they've parked themselves this time.

Once I find the lost soul and lift him out of hiding, he shows no remorse. In times like these he doesn't squirm or struggle at all. He'll just lie limp in my arms, a dead weight, taking the fact that he's been discovered in stride.

In these situations it seems that they were actually just interested in my reaction to their disappearance. Did I really care about them? Would I take the time to look around and pinpoint their whereabouts? Would I make an effort—and, if so, how much? I can only hope that they're satisfied with the perseverance I show during all the iterations of Operation Missing Cat.

# Exit

On the other hand, there are the ones who don't show up again.

Once, on the final Monday in July 2020, the nonpresence in question was Johann. For months and months up to that point Johann actually equaled Moritz when it came to his attendance record at mealtimes. When I came out each morning, he was always millimeters away from the back door. He was the one who, about a half an hour later on, watched me longingly when I made a second appearance, this time to give the roses and veggies their daily water fix. He was hoping against hope for more food, of course. Truth be told, sometimes his yearnings found an answer in an extra snack that I sneaked his way. This morning, though, there was no sign of him at all, even at the 8 PM meal. I found myself missing his steady and penetrating gaze, the feel of his sandpapery fur.

And now he was nowhere to be found.

On the following evening I rustled up some dinner—"Leftovers Fantastique," one of my perennial bachelor specialties. An hour later most of the felines were sprawled out on the back lawn, all in their own distinct space, all of them busy, seemingly without end, with tidying themselves up.

But not Johann.

Others witnessing this twilight scene—a gentle carpet of grass punctuated by self-satisfied, self-important cats—would probably see something cozy and idyllic. For me, though, everything had shifted, and the nonpresence of Johann outweighed the take-your-breath-away wonder of this placid snapshot of time.

Wednesday dropped in and moved along its familiar path. Now it was on the wane, and Johann still hadn't shown his face.

So what happened? My imagination went into overdrive. A car ran him over on Blackstone Avenue; he crossed swords with a feral dog somewhere close by; he felt sick and just crept off to a secluded place to meet his end. There's something eerie and unsettling about not knowing and never knowing. If I had his lifeless remains in front of me—the way it worked out with Lorenzo and Falkor and Faustina—then I could treasure the closure of digging a grave and burying him. Later on, I could linger there now and then, honoring him and recalling his charms and idiosyncrasies. As it is, though, I had nothing except this temperate evening breeze and my shifting hypotheses. My gut told me that another wild canine was involved in Johann's vanishing act. After all, Lorenzo was dispatched by a feral dog, and years before that Nanda met a similar fate when two wild dogs loped through the neighborhood and spotted him.

Having a large group of felines for a family, especially when a good number of them are free-spirited outdoorsy types, sometimes makes me think of Agatha Christie's *And Then There Were None*. Her crime novel features ten individuals, all apparently guilty of homicide, though none has been formally charged and punished by the authorities. All of them are lured to an island where a shadowy and unscrupulous murderer aims to exact his own brand of bloody justice. One by one they wind up dead, and in the end there are indeed "none." Who will become the unknown killer's next victim? That's what drives the book's suspense, and Christie, being Christie, builds in some jarring twists and turns in the closing chapters.

With an assortment of freely roaming and independent felines, it's not a matter of being dispatched by a nefarious killer. It's just the odds that face them over the long haul when they live in an area like this one. The rush of traffic along Blackstone Avenue is not that far away, and now and then massive trucks have torn down my own street, tranquil and harmless though it usually is. Some of the cats, like Falkor, ventured out so far that, apparently, they lost their sense of direction and couldn't find their way back to home base again.

And so the tension that lingers with me year after year is inescapable. Which of them will be next? Many times now, when I feed these cats each day, I make sure to treat them with special care, knowing that this could, in fact, be the final time that I can be with them and speak with them. For their part, of course, they're far too focussed on their bowls to pay much attention at all to my ministrations, but my ties to them and my deep admiration for their creaturehood makes this as much a part of my daily routines as actually feeding the motley bunch.

# ENDINGS

What causes suffering in our lives? According to the second of the Buddha's Four Noble Truths, attachment's the culprit. If you're attached to something or someone, you pay a price for it, because that connection will end at some point and in some way.

And so some level of discomfort comes with the package when pets enter your life.

No matter which one we're talking about—a canine like Noodles or Waldi, or one of the cats like Tribble or Lorenzo or Falkor—their deaths slit me open and devastated me.

Part of that has to do with their innocence, at least an innocence that I like to believe is there.

Mourning the loss of another human isn't the same as mourning the passing of an animal. When it comes to pets, for one thing, you can get a sturdy shovel from the garage, roll up your sleeves, and dig a proper burial spot for them yourself. There's something empowering about preparing a grave for a cat that you've come to love and treasure. The way you dig that hole isn't mechanical, and it's not a smooth process. Sometimes you're stabbing wildly into the ground with the blade of that shovel, sometimes your movements are downright plaintive, and sometimes the mounds of earth you're moving prompt images from that animal's life and your own as well. You work up a sweat, you stop and look down at this space, and then it's time to set the cat's remains down into it and arrange it in a way that, for you at least, preserves a sense of its identity and dignity.

It's not really a religious moment. You're not praying and you're not communing with some higher force. You're just looking down at a furry, now-rigid mass and trying to reconcile that sight with the one that you knew and cherished.

That's the key moment: when you put that noncat into the gap that you've created. In some cases I've set it on a plastic sheet and then slowly let it slip down onto its new bed of freshly unsettled dirt. A pause is called for, and I've tended to fill it with a few moments of silence, watching over this thing that had been a fixture in my life, sometimes for many years. Then the second bout of shoveling begins, a phase that's always a lot shorter than the first.

When I worked to bury Faustina, I found Falkor down there. All there was, after a year or so in the soil, was a few small bones and the scant remains of his skull. After laying Faustina down into her grave, I placed the skull between her front paws so that she seemed to be honoring it.

That incident bothered me, though. The way Falkor's skull looked didn't quite make sense.

Toward the close of *Hamlet*, the title character visits a graveyard and comes across the skull of Yorick, a jester that he knew many years earlier. He holds it in his hands and ponders its significance—and, if he can do that, it must be pretty solid after so much time underground. But how could that be? How could Yorick's skull still be that intact after so long? Wouldn't it have decayed the way that Falkor's had? Would there be much at all for the Danish prince to contemplate?

A science colleague at my school came to my assistance. It turns out that cats' skulls aren't as substantial as human skulls are. Yorick's would still have been solid enough so that the scene could have actually happened as written. This Shakespearean moment, at least, needs no suspension of disbelief.

# GRAY

While feeding Momo today I noticed flecks of gray sprinkled through her thick fur.

She's been here for several years now, and she's still nimble and peppy. Getting over the chain-link fence between my place and Augie's isn't a problem for her, and she always leaps up the back steps with ease and grace.

But her energy and mobility conceal how old she is. They keep me from noticing cumulative signs of aging.

The same holds true for Gulliver, whose time with me hearkens back to the early days of Lorenzo's reign as an Alpha Cat. Gulliver can still manage to scale the refrigerator via the kitchen counter without any apparent strain. The fences and walls around the backyard might as well not even be there. They do nothing to impede his impulsive curiosity and *Wanderlust*.

Nowadays, though, more than in earlier times, he often lies atop one of the trash containers, spending hours in the late afternoon sun. His expression now seems more pensive, and when he regards the array of fruit trees in front of him he seems disappointed with all of them. Or maybe, in general, he feels let down about the trajectory that his life has taken.

But what is he actually pondering during moments like these? Even if he's not considering things in a string of words, what sorts of impressions are alive inside him?

Do animals in general, and cats specifically, ever look back toward earlier parts of their lives? If they do, which moments are hardwired in their memories? And do those memories ever overlap with the ones that stir inside me?

In Moritz's case I think of his siblings and his mother Faustina. All of them initially stayed in my house for a few weeks while I figured out what to do with them.

Does Moritz recall anything about those times?

Back to Gulliver. In my mind he's inextricably connected with Lorenzo. Does Gulliver sometimes entertain lucid recollections of his former BFF? Does he harbor any at all?

Sometimes Gulliver lies down close to the cat burial site. Has he just taken up a post there because of its particular ambience, because the sunlight caresses it in an appealing way? Is the grass there especially soft and inviting? Has he settled down there because it offers a lordly view of the whole backyard?

Or does he realize that some of his own have found their final resting place close by? Is he recalling his fellows, communing with them in some way?

Another place that he favors: the exact spot on the lawn where I first found him as a kitten, back when he was a tiny lost soul bawling his heart out in a vast unknown world. Does he remember that, and does he seek out that spot deliberately? Or is it just a weird coincidence?

When they're sprawled on the meditation mat or the sofa, these cats' bearing suggests nothing other than repose and equanimity—just as when they're reclining close to the cat cemetery—but something in me wants there to be more. I like to imagine them recalling and honoring their former housemates—or gardenmates—and I want to believe that, like me, they live in a palpable present as well as a hauntingly real and electric past.

# THE FOURTH

July 2021.

For weeks the days were punctuated—and marred—by sporadic fireworks in the neighborhood, ostensibly in preparation for the Fourth, but probably just set off by people who were bored or thoughtless. The pyrotechnics weren't just happening in the evening and later on at night. They also went off earlier, and they didn't just impact my neighborhood, but lots of others around Fresno as well.

They affected the cats big-time. Sometimes, when I came outside to feed them, they were nowhere to be found. The ruckus had driven them into hiding.

And then the Fourth itself was upon us, and the barrage of random noise came alive with even greater force.

Calling the police was pointless. It was hard to pin down where the infractions were happening and who was responsible for them. Social media platforms were rife with complaints and bitterness about them, for all the good that it did.

When I got outside with the cat food on the evening of the Fourth, the only feline in sight was Momo, and she popped into view only to vanish seconds later when a roisterous kaboom went off somewhere to the north. I finally found her cowering underneath one of the rosebushes and slid a bowl of food towards her. With me close by, she risked coming toward it for a while and checking it out.

No one else made it for dinner. They'd all found discreet hiding places, and they weren't about to show their faces before this latest onslaught was definitely over.

The night was a feast of mindless, wrenching sound, at least until eleven or so. After that it was only intermittent booms and screeches.

135

An unsettling stillness hung over the yard on the next, post-holiday morning. Momo was on hand for her meal, but the others didn't put in an appearance, and try as I might to locate them, they weren't making it easy for me.

I had other things to take care of, like a Zoom class to teach at seven. After that I checked things out again in the garden, and this time Maxwell jumped over the eastern fence, looking famished and eager to let me fix him up with some edibles. Moritz, though, hadn't shown up yet.

A few hours later I needed to do some errands in the car. When I hit the switch to open up the garage door, Moritz scrambled out of his garage retreat, headed out into the driveway, and kept on going. No doubt about it—he was still upset about last night's racket. He padded quickly away from me, and he kept on moving even after he sensed that I was on his tail. He rounded the bend toward the front entrance, and there I caught up with him and scooped up his limp and fearful body. His eyes were distant, haunted.

It took a while to calm him down. He finally got brunch served up the way he liked it—on top of the recycling bin, smack in the center of its faded blue surface—and at last the world looked right to him again.

# JoJo and Ember

Contrasts don't come more striking than this one. JoJo's a longhaired orange cat, spirited and extroverted to a fault.

His sidekick Ember is midnight black and quiet as a hushed library reading room.

When the Camp Fire struck Northern California in 2018, they were separated from their owners, and only later—months later—they were both trapped and brought to local animal shelters that were already overflowing with lost pets. How they survived for so long on their own remains a mystery and a miracle.

One of JoJo's feet was so badly damaged that it had to be partly amputated. He also needed some serious dental work.

Ember was so fractious that the animal shelter said he was feral. He'd lost all of his teeth, and damage to his dental roots was causing him no small amount of agony. He suffered from neurological and vision problems, and he still does. At some point before he was captured something fell on him, leaving a scar on top of his head.

After the fire subsided, some owners tracked their pets down at the animal shelters and reclaimed them. Others never did, maybe because the fire had left them destitute, and as time passed the number of reclamations dwindled ever further. The shelters began to think about euthanizing some of these wildfire survivors, and they developed criteria for choosing which ones should be put down. One criterion they came up with: felines that tested positive for Feline Immonudeficiency Virus, or FIV, would be terminated.

Both JoJo and Ember tested positive for FIV.

One group that sought to help this population was FIV Cat Rescue, an organization that educates people about the misconceptions surrounding FIV.

Lenny, who now lives in Fort Bragg, runs a bookkeeping service up there, and FIV Cat Rescue is one of her clients.

When she found out about JoJo and Ember—or, as people in the animal shelters had named them, Captain Morgan and Blade—she'd just finished constructing a catio on the back deck of her home. No new owners were immediately available for them, so she agreed to foster them until some could be found. This was back in the end of June in 2019.

The original plan foresaw that she'd foster them for half a year or so while new permanent owners could be located. It sounded like a reasonable plan.

Given their condition, Lenny kept them isolated out on the catio, separated from the other cats in the house as well as from Angel, her rescue dog. The wire fence enclosure let them enjoy her garden's charms and serenity while keeping them safe from the dangers lurking out in the woods.

Before Lenny took in the cats, they hadn't ever met. From the start, though, they took to each other big-time. Although the catio had two beds, they always slept side by side in one of them. Now, of course, the prospects of finding new owners went south. These BFFs couldn't be separated. Would someone out there really be willing to take both of them?

Getting the two of them scheduled for dental work took a lot longer than expected, given the backlog that the vet was looking at. That didn't help their prospects either.

Ember was psychologically fragile, skittish. Over the first three months he regarded Lenny with deep-seated suspicion, and she could only pet him using a wooden spoon. His wariness only diminished gradually. JoJo, the golden retriever of the cat world, bucked him up and helped to calm him down when he got upset.

The search for new owners continued.

Then COVID hit, making it impossible for interested parties to visit and look over the pair for themselves, given Lenny's own compromised health situation—her age as well as the tribulations of an autoimmune disease.

And so, far longer than envisioned, the two remained the beneficiaries of her good will.

# Road Trip

In the middle of July in 2021 I went on the kind of trip that hadn't been part of my schedule for a mountain of time. Earlier I'd taken treks like this one in stride, but now I felt antsy, ill at ease. Checking the air pressure in the tires, making sure that I was packing everything that I needed—it all developed in an anxious slow motion. What had been routine and commonplace before the pandemic now felt odd and strange. What had once been simple and straightforward now seemed laced with potential hazards.

As soon as I actually pulled out of the driveway, though, it all began to feel normal once again.

It was a treat to cruise through Mendocino and Fort Bragg again that afternoon. True to habit, I explored my favorite used bookstores at length, including Windsong and Moore's Books. In one the owner insisted that I wear a mask—no problem, I'd come prepared—and in the other one the proprietor let visitors browse with or without, as they preferred.

Then it was time to visit Lenny again in her forest hideaway.

After coffee and a catching-up session in her sun-crowded living room, we took Angel, her rescue dog, for a stroll. Later on, after we'd gotten back to her place, our conversation shifted to the passages I'd written about her time with Tribble and Nanda. We reviewed her comments and suggestions, and then some more material for the book came my way.

Over the years Lenny had preserved all of her correspondence in her file cabinet; she'd organized everything meticulously according to who had sent what. My file in there, especially the letters I'd written to her back in the eighties and nineties, was a godsend for this book project.

Before I took off for Fresno the next day, she also introduced me to her two houseguests in the catio out back. Although she'd alluded to them before, I'd never met them face-to-face.

Now she led me out to their enclosure, and I had my first glimpse of JoJo and Ember.

JoJo was a sweetheart, a grand reddish wonder with friendliness to burn, and he and I bonded immediately. As soon as I came in, he gave me his full attention, pushing both of his hefty paws into my chest and nuzzling me with hearty gusto. Ember, his reticent counterpart, was a smallish shadow living in his midst.

A week later, once again settled in my Fresno house, I found myself looking around in my spare bedroom. Barbara had moved away by this time, and the room was now vacant. At this point it had no real function, no purpose. A twin-size bed was in there, pushed up against the western wall. Hanging on two of the walls were framed mandalas that our mother had bought at monasteries during her trip to Bhutan during the nineties. The two expansive bookcases featured a wide variety of paperbacks as well as more knickknacks from her sundry travel adventures far and wide, like some of the elephant figurines that she'd brought back from her study tour in India.

It wasn't quite as large as Lenny's catio, but it could serve. For one thing, there was more than enough room for a cat tree or two, plus all of the other basic necessities for indoor cat life.

I emailed Lenny to let her know about my interest in her two fosters. After all, I reminded her, I was retired now. I'd have enough spare time to take them to the vet whenever necessary. My regular vet was also just a few blocks away—another plus. I'd be able to keep them company for a while every day, administer meds, everything. I had enough cash in the bank to handle whatever medical contingencies might arise. If the other felines around here cozied up to them, no problem—but I'd keep JoJo and Ember indoors at all times to play things safe. If the others snubbed the two newcomers, so what? They'd have their own space to enjoy, and I'd spruce it up to make it a cat home they could take pride in.

The more I thought about it, the more viable the whole thing felt.

# New Cat In Town

With Johann gone, I was down to a mere five cats, something that felt odd if not downright absurd. I've read that people who lose an appendage in an accident sometimes still feel a phantom limb years later; to them it feels as if they still have that arm or that leg. Sometimes it seemed that I now had a phantom cat, a sixth one that resided here in spirit.

Of course, all of that might change, I told myself. Five might even morph into seven before too long.

The year 2021 was stuck inside an unbearably overheated summer for eons; then it learned how to move again. The summer days were finally waning, and the evenings fell into darkness faster than they used to. At eight o'clock in late September it was already pretty murky out back. Maxwell hadn't joined his peers yet for the evening repast, so I kept an eye and an ear out for him.

Out of the blue there was some movement close to the back fence; maybe some animal was roaming through the dogwood patch and through the rows of cherry tomato plants. Figuring that it must be Maxwell, I called out to him, but got no response. Not much of a surprise there—he was probably doing his stealthy "Maxwell Smart" routine again—so I grabbed a flashlight and went out to see where he was exactly.

But the circle of my flashlight caught someone else—a charcoal-gray intruder with striking green eyes. When my light latched onto this new feline, he bolted to the left, as if he wanted to jump the chain-link fence and get into Augie's yard, but then something possessed him to reconsider things, and he just stayed where he was, watching me—the shadowy form behind the flashlight—even as I stood looking at him.

Six had just made his first appearance.

While Maxwell was an abject failure when it came to discreet surveillance, this new guy was a master of tradecraft. A few days later, when I was feeding the bunch in the evening, he bided his time, keeping his proximity and whereabouts under wraps. Then he shot through the yard like a fastball and came to a halt about three feet away from me.

As luck and fate would have it, there was an extra bowl on one of the back steps. When he got pellets of dry food from me, he went through it all in record time. Back in Lodi High School we all learned speed-reading techniques in our English classes; in the seventies skimming and speed-reading were all the rage. Six, it turned out, was a speed-eater who could put food away with consummate celerity, even faster than Oliver. Surprisingly enough, he let me pet him from the get-go; in fact, he insisted on it. His was a sleek, muscular body, and I imagine that, just like Falkor and Oliver and Gulliver, he was the type who wandered far and wide, and fearlessly, throughout the year.

In a way, getting a new cat to become one of your regulars is like fishing. You need to get your prey hooked, then you have to reel him in. Some days went by when he didn't show up at all, but inside a week he'd become a regular fixture, particularly in the evening hours.

But only at the actual meals. Outside of that he kept his whereabouts strictly hush-hush.

Not that the process always went swimmingly.

A few days further on, morning roll call came and went, and then mealtime commenced. A few minutes after the regulars got settled next to their bowls, the new guy swooped in, wreaking fearsome havoc and then more havoc. He stormed into the house and filched Oliver's breakfast—more sheer courage would be hard to imagine—before racing back outside to maraud and pillage from all of the others in turn. Years ago I learned about the Viking raids in history class, but thanks to Six I now have a better sense of how their raids must have looked and felt.

My regulars were now all unsettled and unhinged. Before I knew it, Maxwell zipped out into the driveway with Moritz right behind him, and Momo beat a hasty retreat from her breakfast bowl. For his part Six seemed to be everywhere, hounding all the locals, scouring the area and licking all of the abandoned bowls in turn to make sure that he hadn't missed anything. I yelled at him, waved my hands to make him take flight—the otherwise efficacious "Sh! Sh!" approach wouldn't work this time around, my gut told me—and, finally realizing that my mood had changed, he fled into the semidarkness.

Now it was a matter of tracking down my scattered crew. Moritz and Maxwell were still out in the driveway. I brought out some food and coaxed them to stay put and actually partake of a meal. Maxwell, whom Six had especially spooked, was now perched on the chest-high brick wall that demarcated my neighbor's yard, poised to leap away at the drop of a hat, or any hint that Six might be launching another rampage. When I put his breakfast in front of his noggin, he recoiled—maybe he thought that Six would now appear in a flash—and it took a while to get him to pull himself together.

All this time Moritz looked like he was cemented to the middle of the driveway. He regarded me and then Maxwell, considered us both at length, and then he finally scampered off toward the street before taking a sharp right around the front of my house. I caught up with him, his bowl in my hand, and did my level best to persuade him, once again, that all was right with the world.

Maybe Six wouldn't be my sixth cat after all. I found myself dreading the next mealtime encounter. What would happen then? Would he still be this aggressive and obnoxious? And, if so, what should I do? The thought of getting Animal Control involved even crossed my mind. After all, this level of commotion was new around here, and if this was Six's style, it'd be best to put a stop to it right away. The fireworks a few weeks ago had upset my cats enough already; the last thing they needed was an out–of–control intruder making regular incursions.

JoJo and Ember were looking like better prospects all the time.

# FRANKIE

A few days afterwards Lenny left me a voice mail that (a) thanked me for my interest in her two fosters as well as my willingness to format the spare room and my schedule to meet their needs, but also (b) let me know that Frankie, a good friend of hers, had now agreed to take them both.

And so I was still stuck with merely five cats, the feeling that something was missing, that at least one more was needed, and the knowledge that Six, sweet as he could be on occasion, was nowhere close to passing that audition right now.

# Mask

Fresno air quality has been an ongoing concern for decades, and now, in August and September 2021, that turgid miasma up above us was even worse than usual. Fires were devastating several parts of California, including the KNP Complex and the Windy Fire not that far away.

On some days I found myself suffering from a nasty and persistent sore throat, and I even wondered if, despite all of my precautions, I'd come down with COVID. It turned out that COVID wasn't the cause—the test I took at a local clinic came back negative—but just the air outside. Soon enough I figured out that gargling with salt water could alleviate the worst discomfort, and topping my breakfast cereal with honey also worked wonders over time. Another strategy that took me a while to adopt—I wasn't used to it, and it felt surreal—was wearing a mask whenever I went outdoors, however briefly.

Six showed up again one midmorning toward the very end of September—no longer in hiding, but out in the open by the back gate, attentive and waiting to be noticed. He'd missed out on breakfast, so I decided to bring out some food for him. Before I went out back, I slipped a surgical mask into place.

I didn't anticipate how he'd react.

Once he saw me with the mask, he panicked and headed toward the fence at warp speed. Try as I might to hail his attention and arrest his flight, the mask's ominous powers held sway.

# SNAPSHOTS

As I begin to put together this evening's allotment of words, Gulliver's joined me. He's squatting on the printer to my right, preoccupied with the earnest task of grooming himself. He licks his tail thoroughly, and after that he attends to his left forepaw. The cleaning cycle continues: now he's zeroing in on his back paws and hind legs, licking and sometimes nipping at them, bringing them up to his scrupulous standards. At last, after everything meets with his approval, he assumes his routine pose—head lowered, eyes half-closed, striped tabby tail curled around his right hind leg.

I'm careful not to move my hands and arms around too quickly or too dramatically.

Now Gulliver shifts his position yet again. His head has settled down on his front right paw. His proud tail snakes around his back leg and almost touches his cheek.

His eyes are still half-closed. His ears, upright triangles, sometimes twitch and shudder—maybe he's registering noises and sensations that I can't detect at all? Whatever those are, they aren't significant enough to merit more than a moment's notice. The twitching stops, and once again he seems fully at ease.

The clock radio on the bedside table reads three-something AM, and Oliver's strumming the Venetian blinds next to my head—his signal that he needs to get outside without delay. I lift myself out of bed—in situations like this one resistance is futile—and he guides me over to the back door. The sensor lights click on when I open up for him, spotlighting Moritz in full hunting mode on the lawn, toying sadistically with an already wounded mouse squirming under one of his front paws.

147

Oliver trots over to take a closer look at the grim proceedings.

The minute hand on the kitchen clock has nudged past seven. If I'm going to have a crack at the copy machine before first period starts, I need to head out to school right away.

To save time I used to keep my car—a VW Dasher back then—sitting in the driveway, and when I get out there now I notice that someone's beat me to it: there's a crooked trail of paw prints moving up the center of the hood and then up the windshield. Whoever it was, the prints on top of the Dasher make it look as if he or she did a frenetic victory dance up there last night.

The expanding jumble of assorted stuff in the garage has reached a tipping point for me, and one weekend morning I decide to go out there and finally get it under control.

For a while I was saving up empty boxes as they came my way, assuming that they'd come in handy at some point, but now it's clear that a lot of them need to be tossed. It's the same story with lots of the garden items stored haphazardly in the metal shelving units. I'd bought them in good faith over the years, but now I know that I won't ever be needing this type of fertilizer or that bug spray.

Getting rid of the clutter feels good. The superfluous and the useless are vanishing now, opening up the possibility of the new. It's as if my whole life is expanding. As the dispensable stuff disappears, I can actually see more of the floor and the worktable.

And here, underneath the worktable, there are even more empty cardboard boxes whose time in the sun will surely never come. When I pull them out, I notice that a few are littered with pigeon feathers, some of them bloodied.

It's not hard to reconstruct what happened. Some of the felines brought their prey in from the garden and finished them off here, first dumping them into one of these boxes and then doing what their instincts told them to, conducting wanton surgery on their hapless victims.

Seeing the blood-soaked feathers triggers the cat detective inside me. Although Falkor could be the perp again, Lorenzo's also in my sights for this one. I've seen him on the prowl outside many times, and I've witnessed what he's done to some birds. No way can I give him a pass about these gory proceedings. He might look like an innocent, innocuous baby when he sprawls heartily on the sofa, but on occasion he also has a savage temperament and a killer instinct.

Six has now become a regular feature of my day. He's also turned into Pavlov's cat, which is starting to get downright annoying. The dogs that Ivan Pavlov worked with would salivate at the sound of a bell, anticipating that food would be coming their way promptly. For Six, though, substitute the back door opening for a bell tinkling.

After dinner one night I look at one of the paintings on my wall and decide that, really, it needs to be moved about six inches to the right. That way it'll hang halfway between the bookshelves and the window and make a far more powerful impression.

All I want to do is get my hammer from the garage. As soon as I get out the door, though, Six is shooting past me and combing the place for anything edible. Plates lying in the sink, kitty bowls lined up along the wall—all of them get the once-over in rapid succession. I scoop him up and he settles down in my arms easily, placing his paws good-naturedly on my forearm. I set him down outside, but he gets up on his hind legs and shows me just how eagerly he'd like to be fed. I leave him in the lurch, but of course the cycle is set to repeat itself. He'll simply lie in wait close by for the door to open again, for his next chance to conduct yet another lightning raid.

# Review

It's early May in the 1990s, and the two-week period of Advanced Placement testing is set to begin. As always, I'm offering weekend practice sessions for my AP English and AP German students, and this time I'm holding the three-hour English meeting in my home. On Friday at school I handed out a rudimentary map showing how to get here, and around thirty of my charges take me up on my offer, showing up at around two on Sunday afternoon. It's a tight fit in the living room-dining area, and students are seated pretty much shoulder to shoulder on the shaggy peanut-brown carpet.

Tribble, of course, always relishes these occasions.

From two until five we pour over previous AP prompts as well as samples from the notorious multiple-choice section, reading, tossing around insights, dissecting, grappling. Most of all grappling. Toward the end I introduce the "greatest hits" section of the session—the part where the group gets to parse the most byzantine texts that AP students faced off against in years past. We work our way through each of these head-scratchers in turn, deconstructing them, figuring out strategies for responding to them, going over sample responses that worked well and some others that crashed and hideously burned. The students are often doing work in groups of three or four, deliberating among themselves.

Tribble takes his time before he makes his entrance, but once he does, he saunters from one group to the next and waits expectantly beside each one. Sure enough, many people do notice him—he's too big and insistent for most to overlook—and he typically gets the attention that he's yearning for. Sometimes, though, some groups are too engrossed in their work, or maybe just indifferent to his needs, and after a while he moves on to the next one. He's puzzled, and maybe even a little distraught, by their failure to tend to him. Overall, though, the afternoon's a success for him, as it always is.

Close to four we take a break, and an impromptu game of football comes together out on the front lawn. But soon enough they're all back inside, and Tribble is quick to seize these moments and gather even more strokes.

Almost five, and the session's gradually wrapping up. Those who came in their own cars are quickly gone; the others linger outside for their rides to come. Tribble tours the now-empty living room and inspects it all carefully. He considers where to settle down, and he seems to weigh the pros and cons of a few choice sites. Finally, his decision made, he mounts the sofa and gets comfortable for the next few hours.

I can't help feeling that, contrary to the timeworn bias, this is one black cat that always brings people good luck, and lots of it.

# EVENING

It's nowhere near mealtime, and if Oliver could read the clock on the kitchen wall he'd have to concede that point. In fact, it's barely past seven in the evening. I've made the imprudent error of stepping close to the kitchen, though, so he's scuttled ahead of me, anticipating a hearty meal.

When that doesn't materialize, he's quick to lose his patience and his cool. Now he's tracing maniacal figure eights on the floor in front of me, all the while giving off a satanic wail that doesn't want to end. His frantic eyes lock onto mine, but when that routine doesn't do the trick, he resorts to his other standard tactic. He slumps onto the floor and tries—with some success, I admit—to project over-the-top cuteness.

Still, the food stays put in the cupboard. Sensing that my resolve can't be breached, he abruptly gets up, wanders over to the back door, and starts to stare at it intently, his tail raised high behind him—the familiar signal that he wants to go on an evening constitutional.

An hour later feeding time has actually arrived. Almost all of the cats have assembled out back, and they're gazing up at the door. As soon they notice my face, they grow restless and noisy. Moritz takes a half-turn, sizes up the blue recycling bin, then leaps up on top of it, only to whirl around and stare at me insistently with his penetrating mint-green eyes.

Six has now become one of my regulars.

Maxwell, off to the side, ponders his position doubtfully. He looks around at the others for indications of what he should do. Then, once I crack open the door and come out with a stack of opened tins, it suddenly hits him that he should strike out toward the bowl waiting for him under the apricot tree, in the center of the yard.

The garden's redolent of a familiar autumn evening atmosphere—shadows and silence gathering incrementally, the sunset's rays still glimmering from the west along with the lights from an ill-placed billboard on Blackstone Avenue.

Some of the pets will opt to make dramatic entrances long after the others, and recently Gulliver's been given to this sort of theatrical excess. When he finally clambers over the garden wall and drops into the backyard, the others are deeply absorbed in their munching and chomping, and he takes in the scene like a movie camera executing a leisurely pan. He bides his time before approaching the house, but finally, when he senses that the coast is reasonably clear, he inches toward the back steps. Once he knows that he's caught my eye, he careens up all of them and slips inside.

Now the outdoor cats start playing a spirited round of Musical Bowls, moving from one bowl to another, sampling their peers' meals and, apparently, savoring what they've discovered.

Taken in isolation, Gulliver's movements are hardly intricate—nor are Momo's, nor, certainly, are Maxwell's. Together, though, they form a convoluted nexus of motion that baffles and overwhelms the senses. Try as I might, I can't untangle all of their quirky movements. I can see, but I don't know what, exactly, I'm seeing.

The outdoor cats remain engrossed in their food. It's a serious affair, all-consuming, and I'm reminded of rows and rows of students sitting in the school library or the cafeteria, heads bowed in earnest concentration, as they grappled with the challenges of SAT or AP exams. If I move among these cats now, they hardly acknowledge my presence; they barely take notice of me at all. Their heaping bowls command all of their attention and spirit.

When I get inside and secure the door behind me, Gulliver's there waiting for me. He's smack in the middle of the kitchen floor—his expression expectant, even desperate. Because of those tooth extractions he now prefers a strictly wet food diet, and as I prepare everything just so for him he monitors my actions fastidiously.

Getting Gulliver's food ready has become harder of late. He's shadowing me with excited anticipation, and he inadvertently blocks everything that I need to do. I want to get another cat tin from the fridge, but now he's in front of me, running interference, and if I try to get around him, he moves again and stops things from being quite that easy for me. Ditto for when I take the cat food to the counter, yank the lid open, and start spooning his portion out into his bowl. He's circling around below me like a satellite in an unstable orbit, and I've got to watch my steps so that I don't bump into him or step on him.

The most daunting phase of this mission, of course, is yet to come. Will Gulliver, hyperfinicky eater that he is, just circle around his meal, sniff at its contents, and peer at it doubtfully? Or will he be content with what's on the menu this evening? This time, though, the cat gods have given us their blessing. He dips his head halfway into the bowl and begins, tentatively at first and then more vigorously, to bite into the quasi sphere that's his dinner. Nowadays he moves his head more when he eats, turning it this way and that, and sometimes he angles around to another side of the bowl where eating success is, for whatever mysterious reason, more easily achieved. Overall things seem to be going well, though, so I back away and leave him to the joy of eating.

Five or ten minutes later I'm back in the study, scrolling through emails, when something—a sixth sense, or maybe just a cat sense—tells me that someone else is in here with me. It's Gulliver, framed in the doorway, tilting his head to one side with an expression that's both quizzical and suppliant. He's already feasted on his regular portion, but he probably figures that asking—especially in his low-key and low-volume way—can't be wrong, and that it can't hurt.

So what am I seeing when I look down at Gulliver? A companion? A soul mate? Or is he really just a freeloader feline who wants to manipulate me flagrantly?

His eyes seem to speak volumes, and his patience, as his gaze locks onto mine, is boundless.

As a rule, of course, I stick to a rigid this–much–food–at–mealtimes–and–no–more policy.

"All right, guy," I tell him, as we both head back to the kitchen cupboards. "But remember—this will be our secret."

# Acknowledgements

I first met Anne Bell back in 1975, when both of us spent a year studying at the state university in Freiburg im Breisgau in what at that time was West Germany. "The Answer to All Division," her recent exhibition at East Arkansas Community College, featured her "Collared Cat" painting, and I'm grateful that she's let me use it on the cover of *Feeding Time* and also edited and commented on a portion of my manuscript.

Lenny Noack has been a dear friend for many years, but now she's also become an indispensable reader of my written work. I'm grateful for all of her astute suggestions and insights, and, of course, for the way that she introduced me to the wacky and inspiring world of cats in the first place.

I'm also indebted to Frankie Kangas, who provided me with some wonderful pictures of JoJo and Ember. It's good to know that those two are now in her capable hands.

Many thanks also go to my brother Tom, who helped me get my facts straight about Waldi, our family's beloved dachshund, and many other things.

Several other people read over parts of this book as it was taking shape and provided valuable feedback, including Inga Owens, Bill Marden, and Sergio Perez, a staunch friend and a fine teacher. Above all, Kristy Kirchner deserves special kudos for reading through my first draft in twenty-page increments as they became available. Her encouragement, and her uncanny ability to spot all of my typos, were a great help.

# About The Author

Steven Roesch was born and raised in Lodi, California. After completing undergraduate studies in German and English at the University of the Pacific in Stockton, he spent two years at the state university in Tübingen, Germany, before doing graduate work in Comparative Literature at the University of Toronto. His teaching career spanned more than thirty years and included two years of full-time teaching in Germany as part of the Fulbright Interchange Teacher Program. Since his retirement in 2016 Mr. Roesch has devoted his time to teaching online and completing several translation projects. His previous book, *Your Ernst, Who Is Always Faithful to You*, appeared in 2019.

Printed in the United States
by Baker & Taylor Publisher Services